Queer
Engaged
Buddhism

Kody Muncaster, PhD

Queer Engaged Buddhism
Kody Muncaster, PhD

Cover photo: AliCris, Shutterstock
Author photo: Kristina Ruddick
Editing: Kimberly Beek
Design: John H. Negru

Published by **The Sumeru Press Inc.**
Manotick, ON, Canada

ISBN 978-1-998248-15-5 (pbk.).

LIBRARY AND ARCHIVES CANADA CATALOGUING IN PUBLICATION

Title: Queer engaged Buddhism / Kody Muncaster, PhD.
Names: Muncaster, Kody, author.
Description: Includes bibliographical references.
Identifiers: Canadiana 20250274116 | ISBN 9781998248155 (softcover)
Subjects: LCSH: Homosexuality—Religious aspects—Buddhism. | LCSH: Buddhism—Social aspects. | LCSH:
   Queer theory. | LCSH: Gay and lesbian studies. | LCSH: Buddhism—Study and teaching. | LCSH:
   Sexual minorities—Religious life. | LCSH: Transgender people—Religious life.
Classification: LCC BQ4570.H65 M86 2025 | DDC 294.3/44408664—dc23

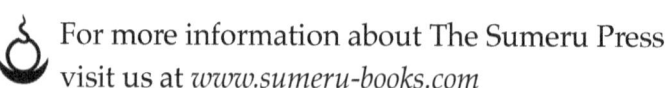 For more information about The Sumeru Press
visit us at *www.sumeru-books.com*

Dedication

I dedicate the merits of this book to all suffering
queer, trans, and intersex people;
I have hope that someday we will all be free.

Contents

Introduction:
Queer Studies and Engaged Buddhism

remember teaching a queer version of tonglen (compassion) meditation for Rainbodhi, a network for lesbian, gay, bisexual, transgender, queer, intersex, and asexual (LGBTQIA) Buddhists across the globe. We practiced inhaling a smoke representing the suffering of ourselves and other queer people we knew who were suffering and exhaling a rainbow light of compassion. Rather than inhaling the good and exhaling the bad, we directly confronted suffering and drew on our strength as queer people to deepen our compassion for ourselves and others, while simultaneously dissolving the distinction between self and other. It was a moment in which we as a community refused to repress our own suffering or look away from the suffering of others. I have included that practice in this book. Tonglen is not just a passive meditation that occurs solely on the cushion. It opens our hearts so that we can act skillfully when faced with suffering. This practice is an example of how we can prime our minds to be socially engaged and how we can use meditation to become queer engaged Buddhists.

Queer people worldwide experience an ocean of suffering. However, as I learned when I did my PhD in Gender, Sexuality, and Women's Studies on how AIDS activist history can influence queer suicide prevention to take more structural approaches (think protests around queerphobia over solely containing suicide prevention to helplines), our communities have incredible strengths. We have huge resources of activist knowledge and of compassionate care. We are also tired. Tonglen can help us tap into these resources, using that rainbow light of compassion, to open our hearts in the face of exhaustion and suffering. This story is an example of how we can queer engaged Buddhism and how engaged Buddhism can impact queer movements.

This work has been many years in the making. Originally, this idea was conceived when writing my thesis for my MA in Buddhist Studies. As I progressed in my own practice and began my Zen Priest training, I realized that a practical element to the book, in addition to the scholarly elements, was incredibly important if this work were to have an impact.

One of the gifts of being queer in a world meant for cisgender and heterosexual people is that we are attuned to seeing the world with a different set of eyes; things that are nearly imperceptible to the dominant culture are blatantly obvious to us, such as the odd ways that gender roles and ideas around sexuality play out, consciously or unconsciously, in those around us. Examining Buddhist hermeneutics, the interpretation of religious texts, through a queer lens can deepen the religion's engagement with its own concepts such as non-duality and compassion. The examination itself is an act of queer engaged Buddhism as we create more welcoming Buddhist communities.

Queerness has received limited attention in Buddhist studies, with most scholarly works constraining their analyses primarily to a simplistic and dualistic question long rehearsed in myriad divisions of religious studies: does this religion have doctrinal support for or against queer people? Queer theory took off as a subset of women's and gender studies in the 1990s as queer thinkers, particularly lesbian feminists, began working through the trauma of the AIDS pandemic and its social consequences. Queer theory's engagement with religious studies has historically been Christian-centric and its limited interactions with Buddhism have often been confined to the question mentioned above. This book goes beyond such questions and instead asks: what might a relationship between Buddhist studies and queer theory look like? And since trans Buddhism, especially in a non-binary context, remains largely unexamined in Buddhist studies, this book holds a particularly strong trans studies focus.

Buddhist studies provides a framework for understanding Buddhist histories and the interpretation of its sacred texts, but it is the sub-field of Engaged Buddhism, due to its engagement with social justice and its applied nature, that offers the most fertile ground for expanding and exploring the intersection of queer theory and Buddhist Studies. This is because Engaged Buddhism focuses on how Buddhism is lived to the betterment of everyone. When I began this work during my MA thesis, I originally sought to write a corrective that focused on queering Buddhist Studies. I later realized that such a deeper intellectual deconstruction may be better suited to other scholars in the field and that my strengths may lend well to a queering of Engaged Buddhism rather than Buddhist Studies. The current book does explore Buddhist Studies in a non-exhaustive way, and my hope is that this encourages further examination of queerness in the field. The book's primary focus is on queerness and socially engaged Buddhism. I explore these two areas with a mix of queer theory, queer interpretations of Buddhist texts, as well as my own experience as a counsellor and a queer Buddhist.

Engaged Buddhism, also known as Socially Engaged Buddhism, is a term often attributed to the Vietnamese monk Thích Nhât Hạnh from around 1963, though according to Fuller (2021) it is possible that the term may have also been originally created by or created in collaboration with a relatively unknown monk named Trinh Van Du. Fuller explains that engaged Buddhism "proposes that the causes of suffering are not only found within the mind but can also be found in society, in political oppression and in social inequality" (Fuller, 2021, loc. 204). I would suggest one could still locate suffering as being caused by the actions of others (or, at least, our conditioned reactions to them), motivated by those oppressors' ignorant minds that are tainted by queerphobia.

Fuller argues that the term is used in two ways. One use of the term describes a form of Buddhism that uses Buddhist concepts to work on social problems, a sort of Buddhist activism. I certainly agree that it is used in this way. The second understanding of engaged Buddhism is that Buddhism can be an influence on society, politics, and culture, suggested by the direct translation of "Buddhism entering into society," from Vietnamese. While Fuller's work is incredibly valuable, what I do not agree with is that Fuller argues that classifying a Buddhist movement as engaged means that said movement is in line with Western values. This colonial assumption positions the West as inherently progressive, which, as we have seen through, for example, Donald Trump's presidencies, it certainly is not. We will dive deeper into such assumptions when discussing homonationalism. Fuller also contradicts himself with this argument as he asserts that not all engaged Buddhism is liberal and progressive, arguing that a conservative engaged Buddhism also exists. This is a complicated argument because conservative Buddhists may be engaged politically, but not necessarily in a way that furthers social justice or that benefits marginalized communities.

There is some debate as to whether engaged Buddhism has always existed or if it is a new invention and a re-interpretation of the teachings. Fuller (2021) explains that traditionalists take the view that Buddhism has always been and must always be engaged. For example, Thích Nhât Hạnh (1967) argues that to be awake is to be aware of the social world and sees the Buddha as a sort of social reformer. Fuller explains that this perspective would see social disengagement as a result of the colonial idea that Buddhism is a passive religion, an idea that made Buddhism easier to exploit. He notes there has always been active Buddhist resistance to colonialism rather than passive acceptance. Modernists, Fuller explains, understand engaged Buddhism as a new phenomenon. He cites Richard Gombrich (2006) who argues that the Buddha helped monastics leave society rather than reform it. Christopher Queen (1996) argues that Western influence on East Asian Buddhism led to social engagement; however, Buddhists have been politically engaged long before this. The problematic Orientalist assumption that engaged Buddhism is modern and Western again positions the West as inherently progressive and as saving Buddhism from its apparent conservative ways. Fuller asserts:

> However, as any historian of Asian history will point out, Buddhism has always been involved with all the people and institutions that make up culture and society

– from kings, queens, emperors and rulers to urban and village education, rituals and commerce. Buddhism has never existed in an ideological vacuum...one could say that the West invented non-engaged Buddhism and, in turn, there was the need for the new category of engaged Buddhism. (Fuller, 2021, loc. 480).

Just like the problematic and overly simplistic divide between a supposedly conservative 'ethnic Buddhism' and Western 'liberal convert Buddhism,' the divide between traditionalist and modernist perspectives on engaged Buddhism may be unhelpful. There have been ascetic Buddhist traditions and there have been Buddhists groups across the world and throughout Buddhist history that have been strongly socially and politically engaged.

Acknowledging that engaged Buddhism is not new in practice, the contemporary term is used to describe the application of Buddhist principles to address present-day social, political, economic, and environmental issues. The Buddha laid out the Four Noble Truths that: (1) there is suffering (perhaps better translated as dissatisfaction), (2) the cause of dissatisfaction is attachment, aversion, and ignorance, (3) there is a way out of dissatisfaction, and (4) the Noble Eightfold Path can lead us out of dissatisfaction. The Noble Eightfold Path is (1) wise view, (2) wise intention, (3) wise speech, (4) wise action, (5) wise livelihood, (6) wise effort, (7) wise mindfulness, and (8) wise concentration.

Engaged Buddhism applies the Four Noble Truths and the Eightfold Path to a variety of forms of injustice and oppression. Richard Harrold, in his book, *My Buddha is Pink: Buddhism from a LGBTQI Perspective*, applies the Four Noble Truths and the Noble Eightfold Path to a queer, specifically gay male context. My hope is that this book may have a broader scope, although I also cannot speak for all queer and trans people.

Compassion and an experiential understanding of interconnectedness are central to an engaged Buddhist interpretation of these concepts, fostering responsibility to reduce suffering for all beings and the planet. By applying these tenets, engaged Buddhism aims to cultivate courage and compassion to face the suffering in the world, to broaden minds and open hearts, and to band together across marginalized communities to work towards an ending of oppression for all. Engaged Buddhism is a call to action to become contemporary bodhisattvas, compassionately dedicated to ending the suffering of all beings, human and non-human.

I have found myself wondering: what would engaged Buddhism look like if put into a deeper conversation with queer theory? Much of engaged Buddhism centres around the very important issues of climate change, war, women in Buddhism, and chaplaincy work. What has stood out to me is that a very limited amount of work has been written about queer and trans issues. I am not saying that it does not exist, as I draw inspiration from many such important works, just that there are very few people writing about this subject. To remedy that neglect, this book analyzes queerness and transness in Buddhist texts from multiple traditions, cultures, and time periods. It traces our existence in a variety of contexts and also includes discussions of contemporary issues faced by queer and trans Buddhists. Perhaps most significantly, it also offers examples of queer and trans lived Buddhism as well as practices that might help folks on their own spiritual journeys.

Feminist Situated Knowledges

Because this book is conducted through the lens of queer theory it is important that I undergo an engagement with my own subjectivity and give a bit of background information on who I am. This is a reflexive practice that has become standard procedure in feminist writing. Queer and feminist writing often includes the judicious use of I-statements to reinforce the writer's subjective connection with their work, grounded in the belief that it is not possible to divorce one's work from one's identities. Often in the dominant Western academic culture it is primarily the work of the less privileged that is perceived as 'subjective,' with marginalized academics being construed as 'too close' to our work. In fact, the opposite, a distance from one's work, can influence one's writing just as strongly and can create blind spots in one's analyses, not to mention creating a false sense of 'objectivity.'

I do not wish to speak with some kind of authority about the issues in this book; rather, I hope to galvanize further dialogue around queer theory and Buddhism, in addition to that which already exists, and I look forward to critiques that ameliorate any oversights this work may have due to the privileges I experience in the world. Queer theory can be extremely inaccessible, which limits its ability to make a material impact on queer people's lives. Buddhist studies can tend toward this challenge too. A marriage of the two could be a recipe for inaccessible disaster. To avoid this, I include personal narratives throughout, as well as applied meditations, which ensure that the book is not solely academic. My intention in this book is to break down various concepts in an understandable way and see how they may be put in dialogue with one another.

I come to this work as a white, Canadian, queer, assigned male at birth, non-binary person who has experienced complex trauma and trauma-induced chronic pain. It is important to note that as a white Westerner in Buddhism with a graduate education, I have privileges that many people do not. I acknowledge that this work may have blind spots due to these privileges.

There has been a long history of Buddhist modernism and Orientalism in the colonial time period that we live in, which I hope to not replicate. Buddhist modernism is the tendency to reshape Buddhism to fit within Western scientific rationalism, making Buddhism a psychology and a philosophy rather than a religion and dismissing its spiritual aspects. Orientalism is the Western exoticization of non-Western ways of knowing and cultures. It also conceptualizes non-Western ways of knowing as underdeveloped and inferior. Buddhist modernism and Orientalism mix together in many Western interpretations of Buddhism. We see this in critiques of Rita Gross' work, who did a lot of groundbreaking research on women in Buddhism, and whose white feminism led her to have blind spots related to race and nationality and led her to strip some issues from their cultural context (Hu, 2019). In addition, the works of scholars such as Roger Corless and Jeffrey Hopkins made problematic assertions of a sort of queering of Buddhism by liberal Buddhist Western converts that imagines Asian Buddhists as always and only homophobic, and always and only heterosexual (Gleig, 2012). In reality, queer Buddhists often fall into the trap (perhaps taught by heterosexual Buddhists) of using non-essentialist and non-dual Buddhist philosophy to deemphasize their identities, which Ann Gleig (2012) calls a form of Buddhist de-queering. These are issues that are important for me to avoid, although my privilege and my being an early career scholar may cause me to make mistakes in this work that I will address as I grow as a scholar and a feminist.

I use "we" in this book when describing the experiences of queer people to emphasize my belonging to this group. I often use the word queer to encompass lesbian, gay, bisexual, transgender, intersex, two-spirit, and asexual people throughout the book, but I also specify the groups involved when it is necessary to make them more explicit. I recognize that there are myriad other sexual and gender identities across languages, time periods, and cultures. These are the ones that I can most accurately speak to (and not for) due to my geographic and cultural locations.

My journey to Buddhism was largely as a result of the queer suffering that I experienced. I was raised by parents who would be considered as culturally Christian but who did not go to church and were closer to atheism. The only time they ever brought up the Bible to me was to tell me that God said it was Adam and Eve not Adam and Steve. During the summer before grade 12, I escaped my physically violent, queerphobic home and went to my fast food job with a garbage bag full of my possessions, not knowing where I would sleep that night. That day, some sort of inner wisdom came to me in the middle of yet another screaming match with one of my parents. This inner wisdom kept repeating, "this is not the life I want to live," and when I walked down the street with that garbage bag, it repeated, "do not look back."

There was a teacher at my school who taught me about mindfulness and feminism. She lent me C.J. Pascoe's book *Dude You're a Fag: Masculinity and sexuality in high school*, a sociological study of the use of the word 'fag' to discipline boys into masculinity. The book had an incredible impact on my life; the bullying I experienced did not hurt as much. Instead, it was interesting, as I would analyze it through a sociological lens, seeing how my bullies had been conditioned by hegemonic masculinity and were attempting to condition me. She worried that there could be trouble in my home and asked that I call her if anything happened over the summer. When I first called her, I reached her husband and asked that he relay the message for me. She was at the hairdressers at the time and a psychic there said to her that she had a sense that my teacher was worried about a young boy. When she got home, her husband told her that I had called. She helped arrange foster care for me and the lesbian social worker to whom I was assigned helped me find a mindfulness-based queer affirming therapist. Once I got into foster care, I was in a safe enough place that the emotions, which were too intense for me to fully experience during the abuse, poured out. Just like my teacher, my therapist used mindfulness practices (some of which I have included in this book) and feminist therapy to help me work through the trauma of violent child abuse, bullying, and sexual abuse from a school bus driver, that I had survived.

I continued learning about mindfulness throughout my undergrad and I used it in various mental health positions, but I felt like I wanted to dig deeper. When I worked in HIV/AIDS, there was a Buddhist recovery group led by a harm reduction case manager who was like a father to many people in the community. We did tonglen, a compassion meditation that is in Chapter 4 of this book, and shared insights from various Buddhist authors that we had read, forming a community of care. I used mindfulness both to cope with difficulties at work and in teaching mindfulness and yoga for queer and trans clients, but something was missing. I wanted to learn more about where these practices came from and the differences between various traditions, but I found it difficult as a Canadian to learn about Buddhism. When I began my PhD in Gender, Sexuality, and Women's Studies, I simultaneously worked on an online MA in Buddhist Studies part-time at the University of South Wales. This provided exactly the overview of Buddhism that

I was looking for. Much of this book comes from my MA research on queer and trans Buddhism.

This book is not meant to be comprehensive. There are much lengthier works on sexuality in Buddhist studies such as Jose Cabezón's (2017) *Sexuality in Classical South Asian Buddhism*. Rather, I hope that this book will serve to galvanize deeper work on queer and trans people in engaged Buddhism and perhaps spark some ideas in its readers just as previously published work impacted me.

While in grad school, I took a course on Buddhist Grief Counselling from Venerable Bhikkuni Thích Nữ Tịnh Quang (whom we also call *Sư cô*, an honorific meaning Buddhist nun) through a free counselling clinic focused on mindfulness practices, and I eventually joined that clinic as a counsellor. Bhikkhuni Tịnh Quang is a Zen Buddhist nun (or rather, a better and gender neutral translation might simply be 'monastic') and a retired Gestalt therapist who used to head an addiction centre. I immediately related to her as someone who worked extensively in mental health. At the time, I was primarily doing Vajrayana Buddhist practices like tonglen, but I asked Bhikkhuni Tịnh Quang if I could take the Zen precepts and bodhisattva vows with her in 2021, and I joined her sangha. I attend her temple regularly and she has become my main teacher. I eventually became a formal disciple of Bhikkhuni Tịnh Quang and began a three-year Zen Priest training program under her in 2024. Like many Westerners, I came to Buddhism seeking emotional healing. The deeper I got, the more interested I became in working on opening my heart, becoming more compassionate, and transcending self/other dualities and binaries.

I remember speaking to a Vietnamese Pure Land monk who was quite surprised that I had a female master, since he perceived me as male (I did not bother coming out as non-binary). He called a young monk over and made a spectacle out of my having a woman for a teacher. He pointed to a nun who appeared to be in her 80s or more and told me that despite her age and experience with ordination she would need to obey the young monk he had called over, who was probably in his late 20s or early 30s. Then he stopped and said, "but we have equality now" …but what he had just said made it sound like those rules still stood. Part of me wondered if he was hoping to get a reaction out of me. It is very important to not take stories like this and make generalizations about Vietnamese culture or Pure Land Buddhism. There is a great deal of sexism in the West as well and there are likely many Vietnamese and Pure Land temples that do not abide by these notions. I include it here because it is important to name oppression when we see it.

Having a woman as a teacher made me feel more comfortable as a queer person, especially knowing that my teacher had been involved in working towards gender equality in Buddhism through her work at the Sakyadhita International Association of Buddhist Women. After Sư cô ordained in Vietnam, her master instructed her to keep her house in Canada and return to it to teach. There were not a lot of resources in this predominantly Christian country for her to draw from, which also made it important that we have her as a teacher here. Sư cô once said to me, "I will tell you as a LGBTQ person the same thing that my master said to me [as a Western person ordaining in Vietnam]: you will have to find your own path."

Because of the scarcity of queer writing in Buddhist studies and in engaged Buddhism, I have decided to include elements of what some might call autoethnography alongside textual analysis in this book in hopes of honouring our place as queer people in this religion and this academic discipline. When I first drafted this, I emphasized in this section that this is not an autoethnography and I tried to justify my inclusion of personal narrative without a sustained analysis as still appropriate. I then revised it to state that I include occasional autoethnographic elements but that this was not the core part of the text. Even though one of my master's degrees and my doctoral work are in gender and sexuality studies, a tradition that purports to value autoethnography, I remained resistant to including these narratives due to the devaluing of personal experience in academia.

We also see the use of the term scholar-practitioner in Buddhist studies, particularly in theology, though that too can be devalued. These rational/emotional, objective/subjective dualisms, which are empty of inherent existence, remain ingrained in me despite

years of feminist academic training to the contrary. I am now lean-
ing into the fact that this piece is indeed an autoethnography rather
than resisting it, because queer and trans stories deserve to be told
in this context where we are often erased and because I do not wish
to buy into the notion that those who have distance from their work
are more objective. My Zen practice has also led me to become a bit
disinterested in semantic debates such as whether or not this is an
autoethnography and whether or not that lessens its value. Indeed,
the subjectivity of autoethnography is one way to put queer engaged Buddhism into practice. Indeed, authors who do not have a
relationship with their work may be the most subjective of all.

Chapter Outline

1: Theoretical Frameworks for Queer Engaged Buddhism
discusses the theoretical basis from which this book grounds its
discussion of queerness and Buddhism. It discusses Queer Studies
and trauma studies, with a particular focus on work regarding
queer affect. Also included are instructions for breath meditation
and compassionate silent illumination meditation at the end, since
many meditation instructions might be inaccessible for queer folks
and these meditations might help with material that could be potentially difficult.

2: Queer and Trans Buddhist Histories:
Towards a Queer Buddhist Hermeneutics
discusses how queerness in Buddhism is an evolving debate that
ranges from claims of neutrality to explicit support, to homophobia. This chapter, heavily revised and updated from its original
appearance in *Beyond Worship* (2022), will begin by discussing
the current landscape of existing work on gay people in Buddhist
hermeneutics and in liturgical linguistics. The chapter will then
discuss such interpretations in relation to cultural values and de-
constructs how there is some work regarding certain queer identities and near-silence on others. A queer Buddhist hermeneutics will
be explored and developed that is highly influenced by reparative

reading. Finally, consideration will be given to the contemporary state of queer people in Buddhism in diverse cultures. The chapter ends with instructions for mindful eating and walking.

3: Non-Binary Phenomenologies, Non-Duality, and Emptiness examines the implications of non-dualistic Buddhist philosophy for post-structural queer theory through an examination of non-binary identity. Also addressed is how the teachings on non-Self and emptiness can be co-opted and used to invalidate queer people when misunderstood. This chapter will explore how non-binary identities can be seen as an extension of the Buddhist concept of non-dualism, as well as exploring various sutras and how they might be seen as affirming of gender fluidity.

4: Trans Bodhicitta:
Trauma, Deity Yoga, and Gender Euphoria
examines queer approaches to understanding mindfulness, especially in the context of time – for example, present-time awareness. Clementine Morrigan (2017) conceptualizes "queer trauma time" to argue that queer peoples' experiences of time are often affected by trauma, leaving them haunted by the past and hypervigilant about the future (p. 54). This chapter discusses the implications of queer trauma time. Meditations such as deity yoga where practitioners imagine themselves being bodhisattvas that may be genderless or a gender different from themselves are also addressed. The chapter ends with instructions on lovingkindness meditation.

5: Trans Bodhisattvas, Queer Practices:
Kuan Yin, Tonglen, and HIV/AIDS
explores the various representation of Kuan Yin as male, female, and perhaps gender fluid. The chapter presents tonglen as a practice that is inherently queer (read: counterintuitive) and explores the connections between tonglen and Kuan Yin in Buddhist literature (Drolma, 2019) along with the usage of tonglen during the height of the AIDS pandemic (Zopa, 2001, p. 13). Instructions for a queer rainbow tonglen compassion meditation round out the chapter.

6: Buddhist Psychotherapy and Spiritual Care for Queer and Trans Communities

discusses what I have learned throughout my life as both a long-time client of mindfulness-based psychotherapy as well as in my work as a therapist, and in Buddhist spiritual care and HIV. A variety of issues such as grief counselling, feminist therapy, and homophobia within families from a Buddhist perspective are included. The chapter also discusses the value of Mondo Zen's Emotional Koan practice and how this might be helpful for queer communities. The chapter ends with instructions for a self-compassion meditation.

7: Precarious Love:
On Interconnectedness for a Queer(ed) and
Trans(formed) Engaged Buddhism

brings our discussion back to Queer Studies to discuss how Judith Butler's (2004) work on precariousness and precarity might reso-nate with Buddhist notions of inter-being. This concluding chapter will discuss Buddhist notions of solidarity in suffering and argue that queer and trans resistance should be more explicitly included in engaged Buddhism. The chapter ends with discussion of the notion of queer-sattvas and trans-sattvas and how we can be ambassadors for change in our communities.

Each chapter of the book includes meditations common to a variety of Buddhist traditions but tweaked to suit queer and trans communities. I have done my best to take into consideration vari-ous triggers that can occur for queer and trans people, and work to address them in the instructions of the meditations, but they may benefit from being modified if there is anything I am missing. These meditations can be used by queer and trans people reading this book as well as by allies such as spiritual care providers and psychotherapists working with queer and trans communities. In short, what you have in your hands here is a mix of accessible aca-demic work from both Queer Studies as well as Buddhist studies, stories from my own experiences, and applied work for queer and trans people and those caring for us.

1
Theoretical Frameworks
for Queer Engaged Buddhism

Before diving into a literature review of existing queer Buddhist work, an overview of the theoretical tools that will be important to this book will provide context for my analysis. Bee Scherer (2021) explains how queer theory (which is rooted in feminist and critical theory) was developed in the 1990s through a collection of works by academics such as Eve Kosofsky Sedgwick, Judith Butler, and David Halpern. Scherer, like myself, sees a potentiality for an examination of queer theory and Buddhist studies. Buddhist studies has been dominated not only by men and the types of inquiry deemed acceptable to them, but it has also been largely the purview of heterosexual, cisgender people who often view it through a Western, white lens. For example, much of Rita Gross' lifework was challenging male dominance in Buddhist studies, but her approach was critiqued for its white feminism and lack of intersectionality (Hu, 2019). These are issues I hope to avoid reproducing here as I provide an overview of the theoretical tools that will be important to this book.

The word 'queer' has been reclaimed to serve as an umbrella term for any LGBTQ2SI person. Nevertheless, it is important to note that despite its increasingly widespread use, it is not a term with which everyone is comfortable. It can also serve as a verb in Queer Studies; to queer something is to critique, subvert, resist, and expose dominant scripts of gender, sex, and sexualities (Scherer, 2021). My queer approach to this work, then, is to critique, subvert, resist, and expose dominant scripts of gender, sex, and sexualities in an analysis of Buddhist works, texts, practices, and histories. A brief description of the following terms will help put queer theory into conversation with Buddhist studies: affect, queer trauma, queer temporalities (queer time), queer phenomenology, paranoid reading, and reparative reading.

The terms 'affective turn' and the 'trauma studies' in Queer Studies are necessary to understand in order to contextualize some of the literature that will be discussed later in this book. Affect studies explores concepts such as emotionality and trauma. Affect might overlap with emotion or be seen as that which precedes emotion. There was a growing interest in affect in the mid-1990s in a variety of fields including queer theory. The development of affect studies in academia coincided with a refocus on subjectivity and analyses of embodiment (Liu, 2017). We see here the way in which the word "affect," is used as a double entendre in affect studies. The body was understood as having both the capability to affect and to be affected, and the work of affect theory was understood by feminist scholars as political in its ability to unearth and mobilize, for example, discontent with dominant power structures (Liu, 2017).

Through Buddhist meditation, I have learned to feel emotions in the body, and I use such techniques with my counselling clients. My Zen teacher has explained that emotions are simply another form of information, not to be run away from or to be clung to. Emotions are also highly gendered and racialized. Often, women and racialized people are told they are not allowed to experience anger, while anger may be one of the only emotions many men are able to access. Here, we can see emotions as an embodied form of information about our social world. Anger can sometimes be a sign of injustice, such as experiencing misogyny, racism, and/or queerphobia, and can tell us that something is very wrong with our social organization and needs to change.

Trauma studies, which could be considered a new subset of affect theory, emerged with Cathy Caruth's (1995) work *Trauma: Explorations in Memory* and this soon became an important part of queer theory. For example, queer scholars such as Ann Cvetkovich (2003) analysed queer trauma as a ubiquitous and often daily experience for queers that creates queer trauma cultures of caring and activism. Trauma studies is distinct in being more about theory rather than about working with trauma in psychology, though I use both in this book.

In the 2010s, another refocusing happened in queer theory, known as the temporal shift in Queer Studies, in which the concept of time began to emerge into a new subset of queer theory: queer temporalities. Queer time is a genre concerned with disrupting dominant notions of chrononormativity, the notion that as queers we must adhere to a straight logic of time that involves chronological milestones of marriage and children, in order to make our lives more palatable by assimilating into the current cultural template of the nuclear family (Riach, Rumens, & Tyler, 2014). It can be quite distressing when we do not measure up to these chrononormative milestones, and an awareness of their existence can help us see through and resist them. Further, Clementine Morrigan (2017) blends the worlds of affect and temporality together in their discussion of queer trauma time, the notion that the traumatized queer mind is haunted by flashbacks of the past and propelled into anxieties about the future.

Queer phenomenology is another concept that will be necessary to understand throughout this work. Sara Ahmed (2006) coined the term to explain how the queer lived experience disorients dominant approaches to phenomenology: "a queer phenomenology would function as a disorientation device; it would not overcome the disalignment of the horizontal and vertical axis, allowing the oblique to open another angle on the world" (Ahmed, 2006, p. 566). Ahmed argues that it is through straightening devices such as heteronormativity, the idea that heterosexuality is the natural default and superior to homosexuality, that our bodies and minds become oriented toward heterosexuality. Her work takes this a step further by using phenomenology to queer the contours of our consciousness by considering how, regardless of sexual orientation, we are all shaped by heteronormativity (Ahmed, 2006). For example, in her work on un/happiness, Ahmed (2010) explains that queers are made happy by objects (for example, boys liking makeup) that should make us unhappy; these very objects make the unbearable suffering of queer life more bearable, but our happiness makes cisgender, straight people, such as our families, unhappy, who then transfer their unhappiness onto us. In Gestalt therapy, a psycho-therapeutic modality influenced by Buddhism, this is called intro-jection, where we unconsciously incorporate someone else's values (such as the idea that boys should not wear makeup) into our own egostructure. We can use the Gestalt empty chair technique here by designating one chair to represent the part that believes this, sitting in that chair, and speaking from it, then switching chairs and speak-ing from what we actually value, in order to help externalize the introjection and discover who we really are. If we are stuck, my Zen teacher explains that we can put the Buddha in a chair and then sit in that chair and speak from the Buddha's perspective.

Adult queers are compelled to appear happy; we must be per-fectly content queer role models for queer youth, satisfied with what little we have, and healed from our trauma, yet a false hap-piness risks allowing the structural causes of our unhappiness to disappear from view (Ahmed, 2006). Piepzna-Samarasinha (2018) similarly talks about the pressure for queer adults to appear totally mentally healthy and the lack of services for queer adults experienc-ing suicidal thoughts. Queer utopian thinking calls for an affect of hope, but Ahmed cautions that this hope must not take the form of a hope that "reimagines the world *as if* there [already] is no discrim-ination" (Ahmed, 2006, p. 113). Rather, sometimes hope can be a driver towards activism, perhaps inspired by the work of our queer ancestors, and sometimes it can seem like hope is all that we have.

Eve Sedgwick's (2003) work on paranoid and reparative read-ing as steeped in an affect of hope is germane to the work done in this book, as I use this approach to analyze Buddhist texts. Sedgwick (who has also written about Buddhism) argues that an excessively critical reading of texts has dominated queer the-ory, which she terms 'paranoid reading.' According to Sedgwick, there are five components to paranoid reading: (1) it anticipates a negative outcome, always attempting to prevent bad surprises; (2) it requires a mimetic imitation of its own methods and only un-derstands imitations of itself as valid; (3) it is a strong theory that is both easily teachable and tautological; (4) paranoid reading is a theory of negative affects, due to its anxious compulsion to maximize literary pleasure and minimize pain; and (5) it places all its faith in the notion that we must expose some hidden, problematic meaning of a text. Sedgwick explains an alternative to paranoid reading practices:

> To read from a reparative position is to surrender the knowing, anxious paranoid determination that no horror, however apparently unthinkable, shall ever come to the reader *as new*; to a reparatively positioned reader, it can seem realistic and necessary to experience surprise. Because there can be terrible surprises, however, there can also be good ones. (Sedgwick, 2003, p. 146, emphasis in original).

Here, Sedgwick is not arguing that we must replace paranoid reading with the reparative position. Instead, we can allow for both approaches to Queer Studies, though to make up for the lack of the latter may require an explicit engagement with the reparative. While it would be easy to maintain a tunnel vision focus on homophobia and transphobia within Buddhism, this book, while considering such issues, also allows for a reparative reading of Buddhist texts, practices, and history.

Finally, Bee Scherer (2021) lays out specifics as to how a queer Buddhist Dharmology could be effectively developed through a relationship with queer theory. In this quote below, they explain that such an approach would require the following parameters:

- Reflexivity: Self-reflective clarity and awareness of the cultural-specific (post)modernist positionalities that queer, trans, secular, POC, dis/abled, etc., Buddhist thinkers inhabit.
- Hermeneutics: Liberatory hermeneutical strategies that challenge, defy, and subvert persistent anti-LGBTIQ+ proof-texting of premodern scriptures and traditional practices.
- Conceptualization: The development, in dialogue with QT, of constructive-critical queer readings of Buddhist tenets (such as karma, No-Self, emptiness).

- Signification: The excavation and (re)signification of queer/ trans-affirmative paradigms, symbolism, and role models.
- Application: The adaptation of queer/trans* affirmative spaces and technologies of the (No-)Self in Buddhist practice including meditation. (Scherer, 2021, p. 12).

My hope throughout this book is to work with these five parameters in a way that is not necessarily comprehensive or authoritative but lays some groundwork to inspire future thinkers more equipped than me to further develop queer engaged Buddhist thought. With Scherer's list and a basic understanding of the affective turn, queer trauma, temporal shift, embodiment, queer temporalities (queer time), queer phenomenology, paranoid reading and reparative reading, we can review and build on the dialogue between queer theory and Buddhist studies to outline what queer engaged Buddhism might look like.

Practice

I decided to include practices in this book for a few reasons. Buddhism is not a solely intellectual endeavour, and these practices can support queer engaged Buddhists on and off the cushion. My hope is that these practices will serve to help readers who may find some of the content of the book distressing and I also hope that it can help ground us as we engage in structural activism. Many queer people have experienced a great deal of trauma, and unique challenges such as gender dysphoria can present themselves depending on the way certain meditations are instructed. Where applicable, I have also adapted language to be more inclusive. My hope is that these scripts may also be helpful for those teaching meditation who may want to avoid problematic language while giving instructions. Readers can also update these scripts with even more accessible language in the future that I may not have thought about.

Breath Meditation

Sit in a comfortable position or lay down in the corpse pose in yoga (*savasana*). If you're lying down, make sure that your arms aren't touching anything that might be around you on the floor.

Begin with the breath. Take three deep breaths. We don't often exhale as deeply as we should, so try to make the exhale longer than the inhale during these three breaths. Notice the pauses at the end of the inhale and at the end of the exhale. Let your breath return to normal. Continue noticing the breath.

Breathing into the stomach can allow us to get more oxygen and can help us feel calm. Breathing into the collar bone might happen when we are very stressed and rapidly gasping for air. Find the place in your body where you feel the breath the strongest. For example, underneath the nostrils or the stomach. Focus all of your attention there. Savour every inhale and exhale. Some people like to mentally repeat 'in,' and 'out,' or to let a mantra such as OM MANI PADME HUM (a mantra associated with Kuan Yin, the queer bodhisattva of compassion) ride the breath. Others prefer not to repeat anything at all. Each time you have a thought, gently bring your attention back to your breath. Not getting upset with yourself over the thinking; this is what the mind was designed to do. We are not getting rid of thought. We are developing a meta-cognitive awareness of thought, and eventually we will only have one thought at a time. With kindness, return to the breath again and again.

Compassionate Silent Illumination

Silent Illumination is the simultaneous cultivation of *shamatha* (calm abiding) and *vipassana* (insight) through awareness of body, heart-mind, and environment. If you have never meditated before, it would be best to start with practicing breath meditation for a while, before trying Silent Illumination once your practice grows. I add the prefix of compassionate here because I want to emphasize a compassionate relating to bodily experiences, thoughts, emotions, and the compassion that spurs from inter-being with our environment.

Silent Illumination is a Chan (Chinese Zen) precursor to the later development of the Japanese Zen meditation *shikantaza* (just sitting). Silence is "nonreactivity to the activity of our minds – thoughts, feelings, memories, anticipation – rather than the absence of activity itself" (Li, 2023, p. 16). Illumination occurs when the mind stops reacting habitually and we return to our natural state, which illuminates the interconnectedness with all things. Silence and illumination are not sequential, they are two sides of the same coin. I find that silent illumination has more concrete instructions to it than shikantaza.

I also appreciate the bringing together of shamatha and vipassana, working with calm abiding and insight at the same time, rather than having the two worked on sequentially. This simultaneous cultivation is in line with the *Platform Sutra*, attributed to Huineng. Chan Master Sheng Yen at one point taught that there were stages common to Silent Illumination, but over time, it appeared that students were clinging to these stages when in reality Silent Illumination can happen at any of the three stages described below. I include them here because I feel that it helps us understand what the meditation is getting at. In particular, these stages help us see how the meditation can move us toward feeling the body and moving past the separation between body and mind. This allows us to dissolve the self/other experience, and helps us reach an experiential knowing of both the innate Buddha nature of ourselves and others, but also the emptiness of self, other, environment, and Buddha nature. The stages are:

1. Oneness of body and heart-mind sitting
2. Oneness of self and environment
3. Vast boundlessness, unimpeded by the senses; binary thoughts fall away and we perceive body, heart-mind, and environment as infinitely vast.

Compassionate Silent Illumination Meditation

Sit in a comfortable position or lay down in the corpse pose in yoga (savasana). Begin with the breath. Take three deep breaths. Let your breath return to normal. Notice the breath for a few minutes. Silent Illumination is not a meditation in which you need to actively try to stop thinking. Instead, we are learning to compassionately watch the heart-mind and be aware of thoughts and emotions. Notice your relationship to your thoughts and feelings. Notice when the three poisons of attachment, aversion, and ignorance arise, and be compassionate towards yourself when they do. You do not need to tense your mind by concentrating on the breath. Silent Illumination involves being open to whatever arises. This is the method of no method, abiding nowhere, accepting everything.

Next, we move into a warm-hearted relaxation of each of the parts of the body. Here, we are actively trying to relax the body to prepare it for meditation and to enhance embodied awareness. Some folks, due to disability or health issues, may not have a particular body part. In this case, feel free to skip anything that does not resonate with you. It may also be difficult to focus on certain body parts. You can stay within your window of tolerance and choose a different body part if it becomes too difficult. If you feel resourced, you can always gently expand your window of tolerance over time, with compassion, not force.

Starting at the crown of your head, notice what sensations are there and relax your head. You might notice the space where the air glides across the top of your head. Moving down to your face, relaxing the eyes, the ears, the nose, and the mouth. Checking in with the forehead to see if there's any tension and relaxing it. Moving down to the neck. A lot of us hold tension here, and if that's the case, releasing the neck muscles. Seeing how the shoulders feel, taking some time to relax each of the shoulders. Generating some gratitude for all the work your neck and shoulder muscles do.

Next, coming to the upper back and the shoulder blades. Having self-compassion for any tension or pain and releasing those muscles. Sensing the mid-back and lower back and slowly relaxing each of the muscles there too. Moving to the arms. Moving down the arms and releasing the muscles one at a time, starting with the bicep and moving down to the forearm in each arm. Feeling the bones in each hand and taking time to relax each finger individually.

If the arms are resting against the floor or in your lap, feeling the contact between your arms and where they're resting. Feeling and relaxing the chest. This might be a difficult region for some trans folks, and you can honour that with self-compassion and loving-kindness. Checking in with the heart region. A lot of emotions are felt in the heart. Allowing any emotions to be there, not running away from them, not getting sucked in by them. Relaxing the heart.

Compassionately relaxing the stomach. We often have judgments about this part of our body due to the body shaming cultures we might live in. Notice any thoughts that your mind might jump to, and without judging yourself for having the thoughts, bring your focus back to relaxing the stomach. Feeling the stomach move with the breath. Spending some time relaxing the pelvic area and the sitting bones, if you feel comfortable doing so. This might be a difficult area for some, and if that's the case, giving yourself compassion for any difficult emotions that arise.

Moving down to the legs. Slowly releasing each leg muscle individually, in each leg, starting with the thighs and moving down the knees, to the calves. Holding the legs with appreciation for all that they do. Relaxing the feet and each one of the individual toes. Finally, compassionately relaxing the whole body.

Now that the body is relaxed, focusing on feeling the whole body just sitting here. Nothing to do, nowhere that you need to go, no state that you need to attain. Spending some time just tapping into the felt sense of the body in space. Instead of forcing concentration, letting thoughts and emotions through if they come, and then watching these impermanent experiences as they go.

Eventually, you might end up connecting to the space around you. This may happen over time as you practice silent illumination more. You might hear sounds from the outside as if they are coming from inside your body. The boundaries of the body, mind, and environment melt away. Maintaining a sense of not-separate, not-two, and also, not one. Simultaneous awareness of body, mind, and environment, all of which are boundless.

2

Queer and Trans Buddhist Histories:
Towards a Queer Buddhist Hermeneutics[1]

Queer existence has always been debated historically, due to shifts in cultural and linguistic understandings of gender and sexual diversity, though the existence of heterosexuality has never been up for debate. French philosopher Michel Foucault (1990) in his groundbreaking work, *History of Sexuality: Volume 1,* explains how the modern category of homosexual was discursively constructed as a psychiatric category of being beginning in the Victorian era. Queerness is neither a disease nor an abnormality, but advocates such as German sexologist and physician Magnus Hirschfeld positioned it as such in order to gain sympathy from a queerphobic public, arguing that if it was some type of disorder, then it is beyond queer people's control and queer sex should not be criminalized (Beachy, 2014). Western constructions of queerness as a social identity and (problematically) as a genetic abnormality may have been strategic, but they are not the only way of understanding gender and sexual diversity.

Queerness in Buddhism is an evolving debate that ranges from claims of neutrality, to explicit support, to homophobia. What this chapter, and this book, does not do, is argue whether Buddhism is homophobic or queer positive. The question is overly simplistic because, as Cabezón (1998) explains, there is no single position on homosexuality in Buddhism. Buddhism is highly influenced by

---

1 An earlier version of this chapter first appeared in Muncaster, K. (2022). "Towards a Queer Buddhist Hermeneutics: Reparative Readings of Queer and Trans Buddhist Histories." In Admans, J., & Valentin, D. (Eds.). *Beyond Worship: Meditations on Queer Worship, Liturgy, and Theology.* (pp. 115-132). Riverdale Avenue Books.

culture and time period and has taken a variety of forms across the world. There is no single authoritative text in Buddhism like the Bible or the Quran. Instead, there are numerous texts containing sutras used in different traditions and these sutras were memorized and then eventually written down hundreds of years after the Buddha's death. It is impossible to know which sutras are 'authentic,' and debates continue both within and between schools of Buddhism around various scriptures and concepts. Besides, Buddhism is more orthopraxic (emphasizing practice and ethics) rather than orthodox (focusing on doctrine and belief). My intention in this work is rather to explore some of the challenges that queer people have faced in Buddhism and to also outline precedents for queer interpretations of Buddhist scriptures in order to suggest that we do have a place in Buddhism.

I begin this chapter by discussing the current landscape of existing work on queer people in Buddhist hermeneutics (interpretations of Buddhist sacred texts) and in liturgical linguistics (the study of sacred language). This landscape is surveyed in relation to cultural and temporal values that highlight silences around issues such as femmephobia, the hatred of femininity, and interphobia, discrimination against intersex people. For a view into how some of the prescriptions from Buddhist sacred texts are lived out, consideration is given to the contemporary state of queer people in Buddhism. This chapter is partially reprinted from a chapter I wrote in the anthology *Beyond Worship*, but is also heavily revised and updated, as I have become more familiar with the literature since then.

Was the Buddha Queer?
Ananda and a Heart of Love

While the Buddha did have a wife before he began his journey into Buddhahood, there is precedent for understanding the Buddha as perhaps approximating what could almost be called bisexual in contemporary terms if we consider his gay relationships in past lives. Cabezón (1993) explains that Ananda and the Buddha are depicted as lovers in some Jataka tales, stories of the Buddha's past lives. In one story, the Buddha and Ananda are two deer who spend their lives cuddling each other. In another, they are sons of Brahmin parents, and they refuse to marry women so that they can be with each other instead. Given that the Buddha married a woman in his historical life before his spiritual journey, was the Buddha bisexual or gay, at least in a past life? Perhaps by today's standards. Or perhaps he was some form of *pandaka*, a Pali term often applied to queerness, which we will explore later in this chapter. Even if celibacy prevented the Buddha and Ananda from having sex post-ordination in their historical life, it is possible that a gay loving, romantic relationship was present.

The Buddha is said to have had the ability to see his own past lives and the Jataka tales were narrated directly by the Buddha to his followers with lessons on the path to Buddhahood, so while the Buddha was alive he would have told these stories about his romantic relationship with Ananda in a past life – denoting a present bisexual-romantic connection even if sex was out of the picture at the time. There is often a fear of applying an anachronistic label to people in another time period, yet heterosexuality is seen in historiography as such a given that it does not even need to be labelled. Queerness is so ephemeral that we are desperate for traces of people like us in our histories; thus, such a label for the sake of ease in rendering our love and sex intelligible to contemporary discursive sensibilities can serve to benefit beings.

Ananda expressed a profound depth of love for the Buddha during his historical life and experienced an incredible magnitude of mourning when the Buddha died. In Volume 2 of *Queer Dharma*, writer Michael J. Sweet (2000) quotes a verse attributed to Ananda after the Buddha's death:

My companion has passed away,
The Master, too, is gone.
There is no friendship now that equals this:
Mindfulness directed to the body.
The old ones now have passed away,

The new ones do not please me much,
Today I meditate all alone
Like a bird gone to its nest. (Thag. 1035-1036).

The profound grief expressed in this passage may be that of a widower. Ananda makes a point of calling the Buddha his companion while also acknowledging him as The Master of the Dharma. Author Sweet (2000) explains that Ananda's attachment to the Buddha was so great that he could only attain the spiritual level of arhatship after the Buddha died.

Ananda is also depicted in a past life as falling in love with a jeweled-neck snake that appeared in a male human form. The man would visit Ananda in his hermitage in human form and then transform into his snake form to hug Ananda tight when it was time for him to leave. The man would stay at Ananda's hermitage until he had "*sineham vinodetva*," which Sweet (2000, p. 17) translates as meaning released his sticky love fluid. Ananda later begins to wish to leave the relationship, and his brother advises him to ask the man he is dating for money, because appearing as a "gold-digger," might make the man end the relationship. When his partner leaves, Ananda is ridden with guilt, regretting the decision. His brother concludes that Ananda cannot live without the man. Sweet (2000, p. 18) relates this to the phrase "boyfriends: can't live with 'em, can't live without 'em." Sweet (2000) explains that this story could be arguing for the merits of non-attached, ascetic life. However, such a lesson could be taught just as easily through a heterosexual parable. Perhaps it could even be a story of Ananda's internalized homophobia, his running away from a gay relationship and then later missing his lover, an experience that is all too familiar in queer communities.

The Pandaka Question

Debates related to the appropriate use of language inevitably come up in historical discussions of queerness, and often these debates, while important, derail attempts to understand queer as historical.

José Muñoz, a scholar in queer of color critique, builds on existing literature arguing that we must maintain queerness as an expectation when reading, through his examination of how queerness is ephemeral, leaving few traces that are sufficient to reach the threshold of historical evidence to cisgender, heterosexual eyes (Muñoz, 2019). While the term 'homosexuality' may have been a more recent development (which also preceded the term 'heterosexuality'), the epistemic violence of erasing queerness from Buddhist historiography on the basis of language, or even because contemporary notions of gay domesticity may have looked different back then, does Buddhist studies a disservice.

It is necessary to unearth the diverse meanings of Pali terms commonly examined in Buddhist hermeneutical debates on queer communities. Many diverse meanings have been assigned to these terms over the years. 'Pandaka' is the term most commonly used for queer people in Buddhism, and its meaning is hotly debated. Buddhist scholar Leonard Zwilling (1992) argues that the word pandaka is used in the Vinaya, the monastic rules, to refer to gay men in a so-called 'passive' role, those who are effeminate, and so-called 'transvestites.

It is valuable to unpack these claims. The euphemistic word 'passive' for what gay communities call 'bottoming' is itself not neutral and implies a femininity to the so-called 'receiver,' as if one passively accepts the sex. This notion heterosexualizes queer sex, attempting to locate an imagined female and male position within it in order to be intelligible to cis-hetero eyes. The term 'effeminacy' in English is used exclusively to describe a seemingly misplaced femininity in men, with the implication that such femininity is inappropriate and indicative of gay male desire. There may be a claim that there was nothing wrong with being gay; it is just those who are feminine who are problematized in Buddhism. Yet can we pause to consider: should Buddhists then not care about the suffering of feminine men? This femmephobia can be understood as a marriage between homophobia and misogyny, with the threat of being labeled a pandaka potentially acting as a whip to ensure that men do not transgress cultural norms around masculinity. It would be cruel to write that Buddhism accepts masculine, celibate gay men and leave it at that without problematizing the femmephobia, interphobia, and transphobia present in these texts. Indeed, femme gay men, trans people, and intersex people have often been left out of explorations of violence in Buddhism, mentioned solely in the context of assuring masculine, celibate gay men that it is not them to whom terms like pandaka refer. The term 'transvestite' has historically been used in English to describe non-transgender identifying cis men who temporarily don women's clothing (though the term is now outdated), but it is unclear if this is what Zwilling meant, or if they were using the term 'transvestite' incorrectly to refer to transwomen or trans people in general. Zwilling discusses five kinds of pandakas: men who give oral sex to other men and ingest their semen (*asita-pandaka*), voyeurs, congenitally impotent men, those who have been castrated, and men who can only get aroused two weeks in the month (Zwilling, 1992). As I explore in Muncaster (2025), Artinger (2021) critiques this list, explaining that:

> …The list of five pandakas may not be what is meant by pandaka in the Vinaya [rules for monastics] texts themselves. We could perhaps infer that such categorizations were existent during the time of the compilation of the Vinaya texts, but that it might be too strict a correlation to argue pandaka carries the same meanings as the five classifications. Nevertheless, such categories provide an interesting reference point for ways in which pandakas were viewed, particularly as sexually deviant beings and the ways in which such deviance is performed. (Artinger, 2021, p. 308).

Cabezón (2017) argues that pandaka could be translated as 'queer,' 'queer man,' or 'queer people,' depending on the context in which it is used. The intentionally broad and postmodern nature of the word 'queer' may be particularly valuable here due to its paradox of being often used as an umbrella term for sexual and gender diversity that is difficult to narrowly define. Cabezón (2017) explains:

> Pandaka/queer is a gender, the third gender. It is also a class of people who are deemed deviant by virtue of their nonnormative bodies or desires. It would be wrongheaded, however, to assume that pandaka/queer refers to "gay people," much less to a social movement that appropriates a term of derision (queer) to designate its identity. (Cabezón, 2017, p. 13).

Here, Cabezón (2017) speaks quite beautifully to the connection between pandaka and gender diversity while differentiating it from contemporary constructions of a social movement based on identity, though we may never know if such a movement did or did not exist. I do, however, hesitate to limit the term 'pandaka' to being solely a third gender as there also seem to be links to sexual acts.

Scherer (2021) similarly argues that rather than being a sexual orientation, the term largely indicates a genderqueerness of the sex/gender faculty, a faculty being a sort of governing part of body/mind/spirit. Faculty (*indriya*) is a term that is used to describe mental and physical capacities or abilities, some of which are sensory, and Scherer may be using the term sex/gender faculty to denote a sense of one's sex or gender. I really appreciate that interpretation because of how it combines queer notions of genderqueerness with the very Buddhist notion of a gender/sex faculty, perhaps combating the potential hazard of using overly colonial constructions. I would add that in addition to the gender/sex faculty, the term "pandaka" could also be seen as a queering of the physical pleasure (*sukhindriya*) faculty, thereby also encompassing the connection to queer sex.

Homoromantic attraction is not discussed much in the sutras (although the Jataka tales do suggest that the Buddha and Ananda may have been in a gay relationship in a past life) and is a bit more difficult to pin down in Pali terms. One connection I can tentatively see in my current understanding is perhaps a queerness of the joy (*somanassindriya*) faculty (though, I hesitate, because romance is not always joyful). This connects to Sara Ahmed's (2010) analysis of queer (un)happiness, that I explore in this book, where she explores how queer people are made happy by that which should make us unhappy (such as same-sex relationships or queer gender expression) and it is that happiness which makes cishetero people (such as cissexist and heterosexist family members) unhappy with us. The pandaka may be seen as a queer person, a way of understanding a genderqueerness of the gender/sex faculty, a queerness of the physical pleasure faculty, and, perhaps more arguably, a queerness of the joy faculty. I hope that future work will pick up where I left off and expand on different ways of understanding this, especially the challenge of conceptualizing queer romantic attraction.

There is also discussion of the female pandaka (Harvey, 2000), the term 'itthipandaka' is occasionally used to mean a masculine woman lacking in femininity. Zwilling (1992) also explains that two nuns are not allowed to sleep in the same bed together. Scherer (2021) cautions that the qualification of female before the term "pandaka" notes the cisheteropatriarchal (Muncaster, 2021) paradigm through which the term is understood. Scherer (2012) explains that there is a notion in the *Milindapañhā* of a pandaka who is neither female nor male, though we may be unable to determine whether this describes a person similar to contemporary notions of intersex or to a non-binary identity.

A story in the *Pandakavatthu* section of the Theravadin *Mahāvagga* from the *Vinaya Pitaka*, which is a collection of rules that guide monastics, cited in Zwilling (1992), discusses a monk who made a sexual pass at other monks, novices, along with elephant keepers, and gatekeepers. The only ones who accepted the monk's passes were the latter groups of laymen, who later mocked the monks for spending time with a pandaka. The sangha was subject to rumors that they were not celibate and were composed of a large number of pandaka. The term 'pandaka' also appears in the *Mūlasarvāstivāda Vinaya Khandhaka* (Tibetan Vinaya). The story claims that the Buddha later banned pandakas from ordaining and expelled those already part of the monastic order. Vimala (2021) notes that the passage refers specifically to banning full ordination, not novice ordination. While one could argue that this story has to do with promiscuity, such positions are value-laden statements which instead demonstrate how monogamy is read into situations where it has no relevance. While the term 'pandaka' has multiple meanings, this reference demonstrates an explicit banning of men engaging in sex with other men. One could also argue that pandaka is not a contemporary concept and so perhaps it is no longer relevant to attempt to ban people from ordination due to a category of being that is hard to define.

There is also the story of two of Shariputra's male students having sex. Since they were not expelled from the monastic order, some have assumed that the act was mutual masturbation, though the Buddha did subsequently forbid a monk from having two novices at the same time, with later exceptions. This also reveals a hierarchy of what is seen to count as sex, with mutual masturbation on the lower end. Zwilling (1992) points out that gay sex is sometimes seen as less serious than heterosexual sex, as it will not lead to a monk abandoning the monastic order to raise children. This may appear gay affirming, but it also discounts gay sex as somehow less legitimate than heterosexual sex.

The question of sexual misconduct becomes a complicated one for Buddhist hermeneutics as it is confined to the narrow interpretations of a text's commentator, and those commentating on Buddhist literature may not necessarily engage in the contemporary practice of reflexive contemplation of the influence of their culturally informed subject position on their work. In the 4th century CE, Indian monk-scholar Vasubandhu argued that oral and anal sex constituted sexual misconduct for lay people, which, by extension, eliminates the possibility of religiously condoned gay male and lesbian sex (Corless, 1998). Buddhist teacher Gampopa broadened this to include having sex near a religious site, where people gather, in daylight, more than five times in a row, and with a male or with one who is castrated (Corless, 1998). It is important to remember that while commentators can help flesh out a text that may appear unclear, it is not within their authority to make up rules based on their own ideas about what is and is not right.

The widespread variance in how the term 'pandaka' is used puts the legitimacy of such stories into question. I would gesture towards the work of Vimala (2021), who put together an incredibly strong exploration of queer, trans, and intersex ordination in the various Vinayas. They explained that it appears most likely that the expulsion of pandaka from ordination was probably added to the Vinaya in the Second Council after the Buddha died in order to conform with the ordination rules of other traditions. There were discussions of this issue in the Jain Order, which banned pandakas, and it appears that pandakas may not have been banned by the Buddha, but that this rule was added to ensure that the Buddhist sangha was not seen as less strict by allowing pandaka full ordination. Regardless, banning queer, trans, and intersex people from ordination because of an assumption that we are more likely to break celibacy is discriminatory and is not in line with Buddhist values of compassion and lovingkindness.

Intersex and Trans Communities:
The Forgotten and Left Behind

The term 'ubhatobyanjanaka' has been argued to refer to intersex people, who have faced intense discrimination in Buddhism (Harvey, 2000). Yet, there appears to be little advocacy towards ending interphobia within Buddhism and there seems to be less work on intersex people in Buddhism than there is on gay people. The Upāsakaśīla-Sūtra,[2] states that one cannot even take the lay precepts if one is "a hermaphrodite or one without sexual organs" (Heng-ching Shih, 1994). Vimala (2021) argues that, like the term 'pandaka,' ubhatobyanjanaka may have been a later addition to the Vinaya, perhaps during the Second Buddhist council in which disagreements over interpretations of the Vinaya occurred. The term appears only briefly and seems to speak largely to so-called 'true hermaphrodism,' an outdated term that used to be incorrectly applied to a mode of intersexuality that the medical model calls 'ovotesticular syndrome,' but that is not what the term means.

---

2 Upāsakaśīla means morality for those taking lay (non-monastic) ordination.

So-called 'true hermaphrodism' actually refers to a being that can produce both sperm and ova, which, unlike many other forms of intersexuality, is not possible in humans (Vimala, 2021). To be clear, while intersexuality occurs in many beautiful and diverse ways in humans, a human being that can produce both sperm and ova, which *ubhatobyanjanaka* likely means, as far as we know, does not exist. Vimala (2021) explains that the association of the now out-dated term 'hermaphrodite' with intersex people may have unfortunately created the assumption that this term refers to intersex people when in fact it may actually be referring to a mythological being. The association of *ubhatobyanjanaka* with intersex people has quite serious implications.

My Zen teacher Bhikkhuni Tịnh Quang told me that she was asked if she was of both sexes. She asked why they wanted to know and she was told that they would not know whether to put her with monks or nuns. We discussed this in the context of if I were ever to someday seek ordination as a monk in a different temple (we are too small of a temple to ordain monks because you need a certain number of monastics to be able conduct the ordination ceremony, but we can ordain priests), because though the rule seems (incorrectly) applied to intersex people, I think she did not want the question to come as a surprise, especially for me as a non-binary person. If intersex people are banned from monastic ordination on the basis that they would not know whether to put them with the monks or the nuns, it makes little sense why lay people, who would not be living in a monastery, would be banned as well.

Regardless, intersex people can simply be asked in which gendered group they feel most comfortable living, if any such group at all. Ultimately, if *ubhatobyanjanaka* refers to a non-human celestial being who can produce both sperm and ova, then asking this question of humans is not necessary and can lead to harm.

If intersex communities are, by extension, banned from monastic ordination on the basis that it is unclear if they would be monks or nuns, such interphobic practices are likely grounded in the heteronormative assumption that monks should live with other monks and vice-versa to prevent heterosexual encounters, erasing queer attraction and disallowing the possibility for intersex people to choose where they live. It is hard to believe that, in a tradition that emphasizes compassion, the Buddha would have limited the ability for one to take precepts and by extension limited their progress on the path to enlightenment, because of their genitals, their gender, or whom they sleep with. While, as far as we know, human beings cannot produce both sperm and ova, if such a being ever does present with this ability, their eligibility to ordain should be granted on the basis of compassion for all, not unnecessary prejudice and presumptions around what that might mean for binary gender accommodations and celibacy.

According to the Pali Vinaya, monastic rules state that if an already ordained assigned male at birth (AMAB) monk transitions to female, she is to be placed with the nuns, and if an assigned female at birth (AFAB) nun transitions to male, he is to be placed with the monks (Anderson, 2017). The Dharmaguptaka Vinaya includes this but adds a story of a monk and a nun who transition to become both male and female at the same time, rather than a binary transition, and are then expelled (Vimala, 2021). It is possible that this could be a form of transnormativity and transmedicalism, the notion that the only legitimate mode of trans being is binary transition, but medical transition as we know it today was not possible back then. It is certainly likely that some form of gender fluidity or nonbinariness may have existed at the time, but this would not have been understood through the same contemporary lens that it is today. If this passage then refers to so-called 'true hermaphrodism,' it would be similarly irrelevant because, as discussed earlier, human beings cannot produce both sperm and ova at the same time, and thus, this passage cannot be applied to intersex people.

Contemporary Queer Issues

Having traced queerness through Buddhist history, a consideration of the contemporary status of queer people in Buddhism is germane. Rainbodhi is an Australian-based organization dedicated to the promotion of queer people in Buddhism, founded by queer former Theravada monk Bhante Akāliko, which now has international chapters in several countries. The organization sponsored research conducted by Stephen Kerry (2021) on Australian Buddhist communities, who conducted an online survey of 82 queer and trans Buddhists in Australia and presented the results at the first International Queer Buddhist Conference in 2021 hosted by Jampa Wurst. The survey found that 61% of respondents felt that Buddhist centers silence or ignore lesbian, gay, bisexual, transgender, intersex, and asexual (LGBTQIA) issues and 55% were reluctant to disclose their identities (Kerry, 2021, n.p.). In addition, 37% had seen or heard homophobia, 26% had seen or heard transphobia or misgendering, and 16% had been told that their identities were inconsistent with the Buddhist teachings (Kerry, 2021, n.p.). Scholar Coleman (2001) argues that "most teachers simply ignored the more sexist elements of the [Eastern] tradition" (p. 144)" when Buddhism came to the West. On the contrary, researcher Kerry's data found that 54% of respondents had seen or heard sexism.

Scholar Roger Corless (2004) argues for a Western queer Dharmology that examines the queer potentiality of Buddhist concepts such as *shunyata* (emptiness) and *pratityasamutpada* (dependent arising). Buddhist scholar Ann Gleig (2012) points out that the work of Western Buddhist scholars such as Corless propagates the view that the West is fertile ground for queer Buddhism while painting Asian Buddhism as always and only homophobic and Asian Buddhists as always and only heterosexual. Such notions are symptomatic of what queer theorist Jasbir Puar (2017) calls a time period of homonationalism in her description of the modern tendency to co-opt queer legal equalities as a barometer of a nation's progressiveness, enhancing the reputation of countries in the Global North while justifying imperialism on the basis of civilizing the imagined homophobic Other. Gleig (2012) explains that contrary to Corless' claims, Western Buddhists tend to co-opt non-dual philosophy as a means of erasing queer and trans identities. Cisgender and heterosexual Buddhists often teach queer Buddhists that we must let go of our identities in order to have a deeper understanding of non-Self and emptiness. Black lesbian Zen priest Zenju

Earthlyn Manuel (2015) explains that racialized and queer people are often told that they identify too much with the body, but this belies the importance of contemplation of the body seen in the *Satipatthana Sutta* on the foundations of mindfulness and vipassana. Similarly, those with white and cishetero privilege might suggest that racialized and queer people are too attached to the conventional reality of identity labels, when in fact, such comments indicate that white and cishetero people are too attached to their idea of what ultimate reality should look like. My teacher explained that both realities are to be understood and not clung to; if we only lived in ultimate reality, we would not function in daily life. Manuel recommends quite beautifully that understanding the body as nature and seeing multiplicity in oneness can be correctives to the oppressive misapplication of Buddhist principles against marginalized groups.

Cabezón (1993, p. 82) explains that given the diverse influences of various cultures on Buddhist perspectives on queerness, "it makes no sense to speak of a single Buddhist position as regards same-sex relations. This makes it necessary to be clear concerning the historical period and geographical location being discussed." There are historical accounts of queerness in East Asian Buddhism. Crompton (2003) argues that Chinese Buddhism likely held queerness in a positive light and explains how Jesuit missionary Francis Xavier observed the practice of male love in a Zen monastery (Crompton, 2003). Cabezón (1993) argues that gay sex and love among monks was at times seen as a means of preventing monks from marrying. Cabezón explains that in Japan, gay sex was extolled by some as "the greatest source of sexual pleasure available to man" (Cabezón, 1993, p. 91). Cabezón goes on to explain a story called *Chigo Kannon Engi* in which Kuan Yin rewards a hardworking monk with a handsome male lover, which turns out to be Kuan Yin themself (Cabezón, 1993). Cabezón dispels the myth that gay sex was simply an outlet for celibate monks in Japanese Buddhism, as such suppositions do not explain why gay relationships held such an idealized status and notes that this occurred during a time in which married priesthood was often practiced rather than celibacy (Cabezón, 1993). We also see this in the work of Matsuo Bashō, a Japanese Zen practitioner who was arguably the most famous haiku poet who was likely what might now be described as bisexual. Here is one of his poems:

A calm moon –
walking home the gay boy
frightened by the howling of foxes.

(*Haiku of the Forest*, 2014)

In the Tibetan Buddhist context, the 14th Dalai Lama, H.H. Tenzin Gyatso, has issued contradictory statements on queer equality that may suggest his views are evolving. Writer Dennis Conkin (1998), in his chapter in *Queer Dharma*, explains how in a 1994 interview with *Out Magazine*, the Dalai Lama originally stated that oral sex was wrong, but then said that if one does not have religious vows against it and if both companions agree then it is okay (Conkin, 1998). He later made statements that gay and lesbian sexual orientation itself is not wrong, just the use of sexual organs in the mouth, anus, and in masturbation, were improper. The implications of that statement essentially mean the same thing, that, in his eyes at the time, queer sex was sexual misconduct. He also said in 1997 at a press conference explicitly that queer sex was generally considered sexual misconduct for Buddhists. The Dalai Lama is not the pope and does not have supreme doctrinal authority over Buddhists. The Dalai Lama does not need to exceed his authority by changing the teachings because the teachings attributed to the Buddha do not say that queer sex is sexual misconduct to begin with. It is only stated in *commentaries* like the one I explored earlier by Vasubandhu (Corless, 1988), the homophobia of which is due to a blindness on the part of the commentator to their own conditioning rather than true orthodoxic interpretation. In regard to gay positivity, the Dalai Lama did acknowledge that we can also understand the precepts in the context of time period and culture. After meeting with a group of queer activists, the Dalai Lama also stated that it is "wrong for society to reject people on the basis of their sexual orientation" and "it is wrong for anyone to look down on people" (Conkin, 1998, p. 354).

In Tibet, gay sexual practices have been documented amongst monks who engaged in physical labour known as *lDab ldob* (Cabezón, 1993). It is also important to note that there are many schools of Tibetan and Vajrayana Buddhism, of which the Dalai Lama only heads one: the Gelug school. Conkin (1998) explains that H.H. Dudjom Rinpoche, head of the Nyingma lineage did not see queer sex as sexual misconduct. Similarly, Khandro Rinpoche, head of the Kagyu Nunnery in Sikkim who is also a lineage holder in the Nyingma/Kagyu traditions has stated that "homosexuality is nothing different, nothing new. [It] was there a long time ago – in Tibet, in the East, in the West, everywhere…if you really love another man as a man, no problem. One can grow spiritually through homosexual relations" (Conkin, 1998, p. 356). This may be stating that homosexuality is not a hindrance to spiritual growth, or it could mean that homosexuality can be a catalyst for spiritual growth. The latter interpretation of that statement could be taken up quite beautifully. Queer love is sacred. I remember in one of my earliest queer relationships just sitting in awe one day of how people could possibly condemn something so profoundly beautiful and wishing that heterosexual people could experience how deep and special queer romance can be.

There have been some cases of rather affirming practices in Buddhism. Scholar Jeff Wilson (2012) explains that ministers of the Buddhist Churches of America (BCA), the primary organization of Jodo Shinshu Pure Land temples in the mainland United States, have been performing gay marriages for nearly 50 years, well before such marriages were legalized in the United States and Canada. Buddhism does not place an emphasis on marriage, and historically the Buddha did not prescribe a ceremony or a set of rituals regarding marriage. Instead, canonical Buddhism would view marriage as a secular affair anyways and thus there would be no reason for Buddhists to have a position against gay marriage. Even though it is traditionally a secular affair, some temples may provide marriage ceremonies because to do so has meaning for the people getting married, and this meaning is even more so for the hearts of queer people.

While gay marriage has become prominent in gay activism, particularly following the height of the AIDS pandemic, it has been met with some internal backlash. Many queer thinkers have called gay marriage an expression of homonormativity, or a means of assimilating into heterosexual institutions and using activist energy that could be better spent on structural issues (Puar, 2006; Conrad, 2014). Anti-assimilationist critiques argue that the benefits of marriage such as having a spouse be able to visit one in the hospital, easing immigration for a partner, and allowing access to health insurance for one's spouse, should actually be available to all people regardless of marital status; thus, marriage equality privileges those who chose this legal route and leaves behind those who do not. While the BCA's choice to conduct gay marriages may be a kind gesture of affirming and welcoming queers into its churches, it also acts as a sort of dual assimilation: assimilating Buddhism into Christian notions of religious marriage in the West and assimilating queers into homonormative marriage, calming the fires of their activism once they have attained the rights (when legalized) of other married couples. Nevertheless, it is still important to the people who want to get married and who may have never thought they could have a religiously sanctioned queer relationship.

Towards a Queer Buddhist Hermeneutics

The work discussed above suggests that despite attempts to argue that Buddhism has been neutral on homosexuality (see, for example, Cabezón's [1993] critique of this notion), there has been a history of exclusionary practices towards queer people and there is simultaneously precedent for queer inclusion. Buddhist scholar José Cabezón (1993) explains that Buddhist neutrality does not equate to cultural neutrality on queerness. There are still claims that the Buddha banned pandakas from ordination (Zwilling, 1992). Despite this, there are also texts that affirm queer identities and practices. There has been some work in Buddhist studies by queer and trans authors and there has certainly been work within socially engaged Buddhism, such as the meeting between queer activists and the Dalai Lama as well as the development of Rainbodhi. There has not been an explicit naming of a queer Buddhist Studies or a queer engaged Buddhism, and this (brief) walk through Buddhist history makes me think that such an explicit naming might be beneficial. It may take the development of a new subfield of Buddhist Studies and Queer Studies to provide a more comprehensive overview of traces of queerness in historical texts when, in homophobic times, the traces of queerness are ephemeral. While such a comprehensive examination is beyond the limits of even this book, it is important that future work further develops a queer Buddhist hermeneutics, a study of Buddhist literature that expects queerness, is done from a queer lens, and sees a queer potentiality in Buddhist texts.

Buddhism and its perspectives on gender and sexuality are diverse, in flux, and largely dependent on culture, time period, and who is translating a text. These factors make it impossible to articulate a pan-Buddhist perspective on queerness or to provide a dualistic yes-or-no answer to questions of whether Buddhism endorses queer and trans identities. Using a queer Buddhist hermeneutics, it is evident that there is significant justification in the texts for affirming queer and trans communities, and at the same time, homophobia in various time periods has led to problematic interpretations of Buddhist literature.

While one could use a queer Buddhist hermeneutics to conclude that Buddhism embraces queerness, one must balance this with a consideration of the often challenging lived reality of queers in Buddhist communities. It is also important to note that the language that the Buddha spoke is highly debated and some argue that it was an earlier dialect close to Pali that the Buddha spoke rather than Pali itself (Levman, 2019). While the Pali Canon is seen as closest to the original teachings of the Buddha, we can recognize that it was written down hundreds of years after the Buddha's death and thus it is unfortunately impossible to know the authenticity of stories about pandakas and other terms that have been translated in ways that they are used against queer, trans, and intersex people. Regardless, it behooves engaged Buddhists to remember that the

Buddha's teachings on lovingkindness and compassion must be extended to all beings, including those queer, trans, femme, and intersex people who are currently suffering under the oppression of homophobia, transphobia, femmephobia, and interphobia in their Buddhist communities.

Practice

Mindful Eating

Mindful eating can be particularly helpful for folks struggling with a relationship to food. Queer and trans people experience higher rates of troubled eating than their heterosexual and cisgender counterparts (Parker & Harriger, 2020). Mindful eating can help change the conditioning that one has with food. It could also be a bit challenging for those with a troubled relationship with food and thus practitioners must weigh the benefits of this exposure therapy-type exercise depending on where they are at in their journey. This is often taught with a single raisin, but it can also be done with any food and with a full meal.

Mindful Eating Instructions

First, hold the raisin in your fingers. Squish the raisin, feel the textures. Rub it in your fingers. Feel every tiny inch of movement of the raisin against your skin. Next, bring the raisin close to your ear and play with it. Can you hear it? Put the raisin into your mouth but don't swallow. Leave it on your tongue. Feel the saliva in your mouth and feel the raisin start to melt a little. If any thoughts come up, just bring your mind back to the feeling of the raisin. Move it to one side of your mouth and feel it hit the skin on the inside of your mouth. Move it to the other side and feel it against the teeth on that side. Put it back in the middle of your mouth on your tongue. Contemplate what had to happen for this raisin to get to you right now. Feel the urge to swallow. Put it against the top of your mouth. Put it back. Now, feel that urge to swallow again, and swallow.

If mindful eating is too difficult, another option is to mindfully eat only three bites of a meal and to dedicate each bite to a different person. The first bite is dedicated to your teacher. It could be a spiritual teacher or anyone who has taught you something. The second bite is for someone who has been kind to you. The third bite is for someone you know who is suffering.

Mindful Walking

Mindful walking, also known as walking meditation, can be practiced informally when you're walking somewhere and formally as part of your meditation practice. Some retreat centers even have labyrinths for walking meditations. If you use assistive devices such as a wheelchair, the language here can be adapted in a way that makes sense, for example, feeling the body move, or feeling your fingers move the joystick on a motorized wheelchair.

Mindful Walking Instructions

Keep your eyes open and your gaze a few feet in front of you. Begin to walk much slower than you normally would, in a circle around the room. Feel every part of your feet slowly touching the ground. Feel the heel, the middle of the foot, the top of the foot. Feel each toe as it lands on the floor. Ground yourself through the feet. Feel the inhale and the exhale. You might coordinate your breath with the movement of your feet. Focus on what it's like for your body to move through space. Feel the knees bend as one foot moves in front of the other. If any thoughts come up, label them thinking, and come back to the feeling of your body moving in space. Notice the anticipation of the next step. You can do this for as long as you like.

3

Non-Binary Phenomenologies, Non-duality, and Emptiness

The on-going controversy around labels necessitates an examination of the Buddhist concept of non-Self in a queer context. This concept is almost always brought up in discussions of queerness and Buddhism because there appears to be a fear on behalf of cisgender and heterosexual people that we are too attached to our identities and a cishetero meditative salvation can supposedly help us transcend this. The concept is rarely used to invalidate cisgender and heterosexual existence though the repulsion that the average cisgender, heterosexual man may demonstrate if asked if he would ever kiss another man or wear lipstick suggests that the dominant group remains no less attached than the subaltern.

Gender expansiveness

The term "genderqueer" began being used in queer zines in the 1980s but emerged as an identity in the early 1990s to describe a gender that is queer or non-normative (Vincent, 2020). Non-binary subsequently came into use to describe a gender identity that transcends dualistic categories of male and female (Vincent, 2020). The two terms are mostly synonymous though there appears a slight tendency toward the former denoting an investment in radical queer politics and the latter being more strongly identified with the category of trans. These tendencies are not rules and the two categories are both radical trans identities that serve as umbrella terms for more specific identities such as agender or gender fluid. There is very little work done on non-binary identities at all, let alone in Buddhist studies, thus I offer more of my own narrative than I typically would in, say, an academic article, in hopes of augmenting the dearth in this field. I come to this work as someone who has used both terms, along with gender fluid, throughout my life. In 2016 after years of distress and confusion over my simultaneous uncomfortableness with being assigned male at birth but lack of desire to undertake a full-time binary transition to female, I was diagnosed with gender dysphoria by a physician who was trans himself. His exact words, which are imprinted into my memory, were "I think you need to explore your ability to be gender expansive." He affirmed that non-binary identities are a real, valid form of living in the world. Though, like many trans people, I also resist the medical model and its pathologization of transness, this physician's conceptualization of gender "expansiveness," was incredibly empowering.

I have since engaged in a dance between drag (as well as other expressions of androgyny, masculinity, and femininity) and a hypervigilant fear of exposing myself to violence by rendering my (gender)queerness visible to those who may not yet know about or suspect it. Even an earring can lead to violence, let alone leaving the house in drag. I have experienced a lot of fear of being read as queer by strangers in public because throughout my childhood I was exposed to extreme violence both at school and from my now estranged parents.

My traumatic fear of exclusion even extends itself into situations where people know I am queer and are quite affirming, such as at a Buddhist organization with which I am involved, where I find myself taking off my earrings before entering meetings for fear that I will not be taken seriously, and it shows up in dates with cisgender gay men where I wear snap-back hats to appease the valorization of masculinity due to its approximation to heteronormativity in gay male culture. Even in Buddhist spaces where people know I am queer, I sometimes hesitate to bring my queerness up. In new religious spaces in which I am unfamiliar, I often do not mention it unless I start to know people in the space very well over a long period of time. I fear taking up space in trans organizations and I am anxious about not being perceived as trans enough to be doing such work. My queer trauma alongside my trans trauma of intense childhood harassment, abuse, and family rejection, causes me to expect discrimination or rejection anywhere I go, especially in religious communities. I do tonglen meditation for all the other non-binary people who feel this way and for all the people who, acting out of delusion, hurt us. I also will note that my own fears and the strength of them, expressed in this chapter and this book, are current to the time of writing but are impermanent, and certainly the intensity of those fears may decrease over time and I may find myself being more visibly queer in the years to come.

One of the few times in my life that I have ever felt truly seen as a non-binary person was when another non-binary assigned male at birth person, one of the few whom I have ever met in my life, talked about discovering their non-binary identity through drag after not feeling they fit in with gay men. Chills ran through my body as this person described verbatim my own affective experience. Those same chills ran through my body during each piece that I read on Kuan Yin as I began doing research for this book. I cannot speak to binary trans identity in the same way that I can speak to my own non-binary experience. As is customary in Queer Studies, I am obligated to state that I do not speak for all non-binary people. My only wish here is to spark a broader conversation for the benefit of furthering non-binary Buddhist thought.

Gestures that can be read as queer can be dangerous (Muñoz, 2019). Voguing is a dance created in the Black and Latinx queer ballroom scene that involves a reclaiming of queer gestures such as the broken wrist and swishy hips. In 2023, O'Shae Sibley was killed for voguing at a gas station. I did not know him, but he was from the Brooklyn chapter of the same ballroom house that I was in, and I feared for our community. We held a voguing protest at a gas station for him. I became more hypervigilant. Soon, my ballroom sibling was called racist slurs on their way to our ballroom house practice. A month later, I was assaulted on transit and victim to homophobic slurs and death threats while I was on my way to our practice. My category in ballroom was called Realness with a Twist. Realness is a category where queer and trans people compete to see who can pass for heterosexual and cisgender; for queer men, who is more masculine. The twist of realness with a twist occurs when a seemingly masculine person who walks realness is able to do the feminine dance of vogue; such people are called Twisters. It is a beautiful category for a gender fluid person like me. Realness is about survival, testing our ability to blend in with the outside world. I thought I was giving realness on transit when I was attacked, but my handbag and pastel shopping bag must have gave me away.

Teaching as a non-binary Buddhist

I remember teaching a Buddhist Studies course related to psychology part-time and trying to pass as straight by dressing more masculine because I feared negative teaching evaluations from students. Course evaluations impact hiring and promotion decisions, despite having little to no correlation with learning, and minority faculty members are statistically rated much lower than those of privileged identities, with queer faculty being at a risk of being seen as politically biased and poor lecturers (Kreitzer, & Sweet-Cushman, 2022). I feared bringing up anything related to social justice, especially in Trump's second term, given the attempted erasure of equity from education (despite living in Canada, I think these issues still migrate implicitly). I was preparing my slides and I had backspaced some information about queerness in Buddhism. Then I told myself that it would be more in line with the bodhisattva path to keep the information on queerness so that queer students feel seen, even if I did not intend to out myself.

The attack on my way to ballroom practice happened a few days before a Canada-wide anti-trans protest was set to happen. When I taught a university course called Socially Engaged Buddhism, a young transwoman student asked to meet with me because she felt unsafe due to some shifting political dynamics in Canada. I actually had outed myself in this course because it was a course on social justice. She asked me if there were meditations that could help her feel safe. I emphasized that the current political situation was not safe and her feelings were appropriate given the situation she described to me. We talked about the breath, R.A.I.N of Self Compassion, and tonglen meditations (included in this book) that she already knew. I said that if these feelings are becoming debilitating then perhaps meditation could help, but that these feelings are realistic given the circumstance. We talked about how, in feminist therapy, we try to move people towards a conscientization, towards political engagement, as a form of therapy. This might, for example, be by attending protests (or not attending if doing so would be too difficult, but giving some sort of support to those who are, such as helping make signs or giving peer mental health support after the protest) one can feel less alone and can feel like they are putting their difficult feelings to use. I wish to emphasize in this book, as I did with my student, that while meditation can be an incredibly powerful tool for us to work through the difficult emotions associated with being part of an oppressed group and can help us dissolve the self/other distinction, our feelings are not necessarily wrong; it is what we do with them that matters. Meditation is not a substitute for social engagement or political action.

Queer theory meets Buddhist non-duality and emptiness

The Buddhist emphasis on the concept of non-duality can be understood in relationship with non-binary identity, not to suggest that everyone must be non-binary, but rather, as an affirmation of the unique gifts of non-binary worldviews. Shantideva's use of non-dualistic philosophy to argue that we need not see a separation between self and other can be used in conjunction with queer theory to extend its implications to trans identity by transcending gender and sexual binaries. Queer theory has explored the trajectory of the social, political, cultural, and linguistic construction of gender and sexual identities, and queer theory's conceptualization of this construction can be compatible with Buddhist notions of emptiness. Often, emptiness is used against queer people to devalue our identities. I want to be clear that emptiness does not mean that something does not conventionally exist. Here, we are simply noticing how interesting it is that while gender and sexual diversity have always existed, the way we conceptualize these topics as, for example, identities, changes across time periods and cultures. These identities are important to us and the history of their construction can also unearth the construction of the more privileged identities of cisgender and heterosexual people. Judith Butler (1991) argues that gender is performative, which is often misunderstood to mean that all gender is drag. What is meant by the use of the term 'performative' is that gender is reified through its own repetition and constructed through discourse and language in a specific time period. This is somewhat similar to Michel Foucault's (1990) discussion of how "the homosexual" was linguistically produced as a category of being, which actually came into language before the term 'heterosexual' was eventually coined as its opposite. In unearthing the discursive construction of homosexuality, Foucault, a queer person himself, is not denying the validity of homosexuality just as Butler, a non-binary person, is not attempting to invalidate trans identity. Rather, the two authors are exploring how the concepts as we have come to know them today have been developed in language in a particular time period and have social, political, and medicalized connotations. This is resonant of our discussion earlier in this book about our attempts to trace queerness in the Pali language.

Butler argues that drag is not an imitative copy of another gender[3] but rather it "enacts the very structure of impersonation by which *any gender* is assumed…*gender is a kind of imitation for which there is no original*" (Butler, 1991, p. 21, emphasis in original) explaining that it is through daily repetition across thousands of years that gender as we know it today reconstitutes itself. Similarly, they discuss how homosexuality is seen as a bad copy of heterosexuality,

---

3 It is also worth noting that a minority of drag performers actually do drag of the same gender they were assigned at birth (for example, the cisgender woman drag queen Sigourney Beaver who appeared on the horror-drag reality competition television show *The Boulet Brothers' Dragula*), which furthers Butler's argument. In such instances, drag performers often exaggerate masculinity or femininity in their clothing and performance.

even though the term 'homosexual' came first in language, an approximation to which it can never quite reach, explaining:

> Heterosexuality here presupposes homosexuality. Furthermore, if the homosexual *as* copy *precedes* the heterosexual as *origin*, then it seems only fair to concede that the copy comes before the origin, and that homosexuality is thus the origin, and heterosexuality the copy. But simple inversions are not really possible. For it is only *as* a copy that homosexuality can be argued to *precede* heterosexuality as the origin. (Butler, 1991, p. 22, emphasis in original)

Butler's work destabilizes the copy/origin dualism that is at the heart of naturalistic arguments around cisgender and heterosexual hegemony. Their work lends itself well to the newly developed field of queer ecologies as we divest from biological determinism, a perspective that always positions queer and trans as, even implicitly, a biological defect. The search for biological origin is rooted in eugenics with the underlying premises of cishetero as default and of eradicating queerness. This can be related to Buddhist notions of codependent arising that explain that all things have interrelated causes and conditions. The concept of heterosexuality as a linguistic and social category arose as the supposed opposite to homosexuality.

There can also be a search for origin in karma. Ocha (2023) surveyed Thai *kathoey* sex workers, *kathoey* being a non-cisgender form of identity (though Ocha [2023] argues that it is more of a collection of identities), unique to Cambodia, Laos, and Thailand, on their relationship to religion, gender, and sexuality. The majority of respondents felt that they were born as *kathoey* due to bad karma, internalizing negativity toward gender diverse people. On the other hand, they also used non-essentialist philosophies in Buddhism for self-empowerment. In the *Acintita Sutta* (AN 4.77), the Buddha stated that the results of karma should not be speculated about, for doing so can cause madness and frustration. No one can tell you what your karma is or what has led to your current situation. In the *Samyutta Nikaya* (S.iv. 230) the Buddha taught that not everything is due to karma. Things can occur due to bodily elements, the weather, behaviour, external sources, or karma. My teacher once stated: the only bad karma is things that you wish were not happening, meaning that things become characterized as having to do with bad karma because we have labelled the situation itself as bad or unwanted. If we apply that to queerness, then when we experience internalized queerphobia, we may think that our queerness is due to bad past karma, but when we see queerness as a gift, it becomes due to good past karma. Many of the participants in Ocha's (2023) study saw their clothing as simply a shelter for the body and reached deep, spiritual understandings of gender.

The distinction between conventional and ultimate realities can be helpful in teasing out the relevance of the above theoretical work while avoiding the risk of invalidating contemporary identity categories. These two truths exist in both Theravada and Mahayana Buddhism, though they were most fully explored by Nagarjuna (Garfield, 2002), who founded the Madhyamaka school. Conventional reality, also known as relative reality, is that which we see in front of us, our taken-for-granted understandings of the world. Ultimate reality, also known as absolute reality, is non-dualistic, empty, and boundless.

If we look deeply, we can realize that there is no true distinction, that we need both, and that the two are interdependent, but this linguistic distinction can aid us in ensuring that Buddhist social justice aims are not minimized through false notions of ultimate truth on behalf of more privileged practitioners. Zenju Earthlyn Manuel (2015), the first Black person to receive Dharma transmission in Suzuki Roshi's Soto Zen lineage, is a lesbian Zen priest who explores this more deeply in her book *The Way of Tenderness: Awakening through race, sexuality, and gender*. Absolute truth can be misunderstood and used to maintain whiteness and heterosexual hegemony through the misrepresentation of non-Self and non-duality, but the absolute can only be realized through the relative. Manuel explains that the *Satipaṭṭhāna Sutta* prescribes the practice of mindfulness of the body and that we cannot be disembodied selves, ignoring our identities for the sake of some higher spirituality. Our relative experiences of the body are marked by social experiences of race, gender, and sexuality within a historical and cultural context. Manuel argues that we must not create a hierarchy between spiritual awakening and social identity and must instead understand deeply the inseparability of the relative and absolute, explore multiplicity in oneness, and understand that sameness does not erase difference.

A queer Buddhist Studies can consider sexuality and gender from the non-dual position, disentangling the binaries of male/ female and heterosexual/homosexual that are so often used in attempts to write bisexual and non-binary people out of existence, through understanding the emptiness of these categories. For something to be empty does not mean that it does not hold real meaning for people, otherwise this could be misapplied to harm binary trans people just as non-Self has been continually used in attempts to try to convince queer Buddhists to divest from their queer identities and, by extension, to depoliticize our activism. On the conventional level these are real categories that have meaning, and these categories are sometimes helpful for queer political aims. On the ultimate level we can allow for a deeper understanding of their histories and fluidity, and this ultimate understanding enables an exploration of differences in queer epistemologies across cultures. Here, we want to avoid the dominance of Western ways of knowing, though a relative term may be applied with acknowledgment of its limitations and contextualization for the purposes of writing an English language book.

Like all concepts in Buddhism, non-Self is an experiential tool for mind training rather than a denial of the relative existence of beings who are required to self-label for the sake of cultural intelligibility, though it may evidently be mis-appropriated. José Muñoz's (2019) work on queer ephemera in the archives argues that we must maintain queerness as an expectation in reading history given the dominance of heteronormative assumptions that allow even images of men kissing to be labeled by historians as "best friends." It is because of the ephemerality that has been forced on queer

existence in the archives that we are put into the position of defend-
ing the queer self. We can again return to Butler's (1991) discussion
on which came linguistically first, but it may be more productive to
instead reassert the need for conventional and ultimate distinctions
in addition to compassion on the part of the cisgender, heterosexual people who feel compelled to remind queers of the non-Self. It
may be more productive for cisgender, heterosexual practitioners
to work on empathizing with the experience of the erasure of an
important part of one's life. We will discuss this in the context of
deity yoga in Chapter 4.

Gender Fluidity in the Sutras

In Muncaster (2022) I examined how Eve Sedgwick's (2003) work
on reparative reading can be used in a queer Buddhist hermeneutics. Below I expand on that work by locating it specifically in a
non-binary Buddhist hermeneutics, not as the only way of queer
liturgical interpretation but as one of many possibilities that deserve representation. In the *Vimalakīrti Sutra*, Shariputra asks a
Goddess why she does not transition from a female body to a male
one. Some might assume that this is due to Shariputra's misogynistic beliefs about women not being able to achieve high levels
of attainment, a feminist interpretation that I would not dispute,
but I will discuss an additional and simultaneous possibility. The
Goddess explains that although she has searched for her female
form for twelve long years, she has still not found it. She then uses
her powers to transform Shariputra into a woman and she takes
the form of Shariputra's old body. Then she asks Shariputra why
Shariputra does not transition to male. Shariputra is confused. The
Goddess then states, "the Buddha teaches that all phenomena are
neither male nor female" (Watson, 1997, p. 91). Cypress Atlas (2019)
examines the reparative potential for this sutra to be read in a trans
context, allowing for an understanding of non-binary identities as
an expression of the emptiness of all things. Indeed, non-binary
people may have access to a higher, experiential knowledge of the
construction of gender.

Paranoid reading reads solely for critique. This sutra can be explored as a teaching on misogyny, which is not to say that such readers are literally paranoid – Sedgwick presumably did not realize how loaded with affect that term is. Reparative reading would consider such critique valid and would also allow for an additional possibility: that this text holds a non-binary potentiality. In my earlier work published in an anthology on queer religion, *Beyond Worship* (Muncaster, 2022) I suggested that the reader consider Zwilling's (1992) assertion that the word 'pandaka,' may be related to ideas of lacking maleness, though I cautioned that one should consider the culture in which the translator of that term grew up. I then asked if, given that even a hint of femininity qualifies a man as effeminate to the homophobic eye, does this temporary drag not make Shariputra a pandaka? Notions of masculinity may have been different during that time period in the Global South, but still present. I would like to invite consideration of a more non-binary or, even more specifically, gender fluid perspective.

Unlike the Goddess, Shariputra does not have the spiritual power to transform his gender. One might give thought to the notion that while there is a relative physical and social change in gender, trans phenomenology may be more akin to a coming into who one really is and living this through outward expression. We can avoid falling into dualistic conceptions by understanding that in a conventional sense, Shariputra's gender is as important to him as a trans person's, noted by his affect of confusion – an affect that is continually applied to trans people (even those who are not confused but are rather quite certain of their identities) and seen in this instance applied to a cisgender person. On the ultimate level, these notions are, as Judith Butler (1988) argues, performative (meaning constructed through discourse not simply a performance), or empty.

Sometimes for non-binary people (myself included) and for those who are not seeking medical transition, it can feel unclear what to do to alleviate gender dysphoria. Shariputra goes through a similar affective experience of confusion; he does not know what to do when the Goddess changes his form. When I told my story about my journey of discovering my non-binary gender to a binary trans man, he said that while he shared some similarities, what was different is that he did not share the affect of confusion that I experienced while trying to figure out my gender identity. He knew that he was male, and his only confusion was with how to navigate trans care services. I would not dare universalize the experiences from that conversation, but it may be safe to say that perhaps an affective experience of confusion due to a lack of non-binary vocabulary, as well as a lack of a rubric for transition options,[4] may be a phenomenon particularly challenging for gender fluid people. There is a lack of discussion of non-binary identities and what discourse there is on transness in the dominant culture, medicine, media, and education, is imbued with transnormative notions of what a trans experience is supposed to look like, coupled with a transmedicalism that problematically presents medical binary transition as the only legitimate way to be trans. This certainly left me feeling confused. We can extend Butler's (1991) work on the challenge of the copy/original binary to trans experience and complicate it further by noting that regardless of which came first linguistically, there is nothing even to work from as a non-binary person seeking to express oneself. In the context of gender performativity, it is unclear what gendered actions to repeat in the non-binary body due to the purposeful and paradoxical lack of specificity of the term.

In Muncaster (2022), I undertook an examination of trans possibilities in the Devadatta chapter of the *Lotus Sutra* (Reeves, 2008) using similar methods of reparative reading and queer Buddhist hermeneutics. I will expand on that analysis here to consider it in the context of a phenomenology of gender fluidity rather than solely in the binary trans context. In the *Lotus Sutra*, the bodhisattva of wisdom, Manjushri, is said to have approached Shariputra stating that the eight-year-old daughter of a dragon king has reached

---

4 Here, I am not suggesting that all binary trans people want to or should undergo every medical option for transition. Rather, I am stating that it may be less clear for non-binary people what paths to take as we navigate ways to express ourselves.

Buddhahood. Shariputra claims that this is not possible because he believes women cannot attain enlightenment. When the dragon king's daughter appears, she gifts a jewel to Shakyamuni Buddha, spontaneously transitions to male, and becomes a Buddha. In Muncaster (2022), I explain that we can use a reparative reading of this story to problematize the sexism in Shariputra's statement but, rather than stopping at that, we can read how it allows for trans possibilities. Balkwill (2021) explains that readers of the sutra may be left questioning whether the daughter of the Dragon King transitioned to male as a pre-requisite to Buddhahood or if it was an expression of Buddhahood already attained. Balkwill (2021) discusses how the great commentator Nichiren saw the sutra as affirming the ability of women to attain Buddhahood simply through faith in the sutra itself. Indeed, as Abé (2015) points out, the *Womb Sutra* explains that "Mara, Brahma, Indra, and women as well, without abandoning their bodies, without taking up other bodies, and in their apparent current bodies, they are capable of attaining Buddhahood" (Abé, 2015, p. 38). This could perhaps be applied to trans and gender fluid bodies as well. Balkwill (2021) argues that stories such as *The Daughter of the Dragon King* form a literary subgenre that concerns the ultimate and conventional understandings of the realities of bodies. She discusses how she found approximately twenty sutras of young women from medieval China who are advanced Buddhist practitioners who lecture the Buddha's disciples on the emptiness of physical forms, question the Buddha on issues related to women, and often choose to take male bodies in spectacular demonstrations of their supernatural abilities and encourage other female followers to also do so. She explains that these texts often use male chauvinism to demonstrate examples of conventional knowledge.

The misogynistic views attributed to Shariputra in these sutras are shared by popular Buddhist authors such as Shantideva, who writes at Bca.X.30 "may all those in the world as women make progress, becoming men" (p. 141). Here, I wish to expand on Muncaster (2022) by arguing that it is not solely a binary transition from female to male that is implicitly condoned in the Devadatta chapter or in the *Bodhicharyavatara*. Rather, these writings also lend them-selves well to exposing the impermanent and often fluid nature of gender. While gender may be phenomenologically fluid for many gender fluid people, it can be fluid in the context of future lives for cisgender people, but that is not all. I also do have some hesitation about using these texts to make a case for gender fluidity because it is also important to me to acknowledge the harm that can be and has been done to women in Buddhism as a result of problematic discourse around their spiritual capabilities. I am not saying that "the" true meaning behind these texts is to advocate for gender fluidity and that there is not sexism inherent in them; rather, I am saying that it is one meaning that we can extract from these texts which unfortunately are texts that also have the potential for harm.

Renowned non-binary author Kate Bornstein (2013) writes in the second edition of *My New Gender Workbook: A Step-by-Step Guide to Achieving World Peace Through Gender Anarchy and Sex Positivity* that everyone, including cis people, is in constant gender transition. This could be a transition from, for example, girlhood to mother-hood or from dressing as a goth to a prep. I saw Bornstein give a talk in Halifax, Nova Scotia in 2016, titled *Trans, just for the fun of it*. They explained that they had recently become heavily influenced by Tibetan Buddhism's wisdom and compassion, and especially its distinction between conventional and ultimate truth in the context of gender. They encouraged us to detach from our convictions and to consider our truths about gender to be arguable and relative just as the dominant views on gender are likewise arguable and rela-tive. I asked them: "the concept of gender has harmed a lot of peo-ple. At the same time, it has a real meaning for binary trans people who work hard to be recognized as their gender. Do you think we should get rid of gender?" They explained that in the first edition of their earlier work *Gender Outlaw* (Bornstein, 1994) they would have said we should transcend gender as a concept but now they think that we should play with it and have fun with it since it is not going anywhere anytime soon.

Years after Bornstein's talk, I am moving toward trying to have fun with and enjoy that part of me. There have been times when drag provided this outlet, allowing me to explore clothing items and makeup that were forbidden to me growing up. The ballroom scene and voguing community that welcomed me has also provided this. Preparing campy effects in my house and competing in vogue, runway, and realness competitions provided me with a huge community of queer people to explore gender fluidity, putting an end to the isolation I was feeling at the time.

In Muncaster (2022), I explained that reparative reading is guided by an affect of hope (Sedgwick, 2003) and that due to the ephemerality of queerness, we must grasp mere traces of our existence in Buddhist texts. My intention with this chapter has been to expand on my earlier views in a few ways: a) I am no longer interested in catering to the notion that these are "mere traces" of our existence, and I wish to propose that we read with transness as an expectation (just as Muñoz [2019] discusses doing so for queerness) given that, as Bornstein points out, we are all constantly in transition and we are accustomed to reading with cisgenderness as an expectation; b) I call for a trans Buddhism that centralizes gender fluidity as much as it does binary transness in its work; and c) I want to encourage a trans Buddhist hermeneutics that reframes these temporal visits to the past to be a way of honouring our trancestors rather than focusing on proving our historical existence to cisgender people.

4

Trans Bodhichitta:
Trauma, Deity Yoga, and Gender Euphoria

Queer Studies is haunted by the past. Ann Cvetkovich's (2003) work on trauma invokes the metaphorical ghosts of women AIDS activists who had nearly been erased from AIDS historiography. Morrigan's (2017) work on queer trauma time shows how queer theory revisits the traumatic past with an anxious hypervigilance that informs perspectives on queer futurities. Heather Love's (2009) work highlights the importance of "negative"[5] queer affects. These authors argue for a consideration of how painful feelings from the past haunt the present. Rather than indulging in the urge to use modernist mindfulness to overlook the past, we can observe how memories show up in the present. This chapter examines critical work on trauma in Queer Studies with a particular focus on trans affect. I then discuss what trans realities can teach us about Buddhist meditation.

Trans trauma and time

There is a temporality (a relationship with time) to queer trauma that impacts the cognitive and affective experiences of one's world. Morrigan (2017) discusses their own lived reality as a non-binary person living with complex trauma in their conceptualization of queer trauma time. They discuss how the queerly traumatized engage in a form of cognitive and affective mental time travel through flashbacks, nightmares, and hypervigilance (Morrigan, 2017) but they argue for an embracing of this in line with the values of Crip

---

5 I prefer to say "challenging," rather "negative" affects or emotions.

and Mad disability justice activism rather than carrying a notion that this way of being is wrong. Crip and Mad activists reclaim the use of the word "cripple," and "mad," or "crazy," in a form of critical disability justice that sees disability as another of many beautiful ways of being.

As someone who has experienced complex trauma, there have been times in my life where I have been among the queerly traumatized who resist linear time by refusing (often against my own will) to exist solely in the present moment, haunted by flashbacks from the past and anxieties about the future. When I was introduced to the secularized, Buddhist modernist mindfulness meditation movement, I saw meditation as a sort of temporary cure, a way to build my skills to eventually stay in the present moment. Bhikkhu Bodhi (2013) problematizes this understanding of mindfulness as presented in Jon Kabat-Zinn's mindfulness-based stress reduction as reductionist but still of benefit to some beings. Bodhi explains that the term 'sati,' which is often referred to as mindfulness, originally meant 'memory.' The Buddha ascribed to it a secondary meaning and it is thus used in two primary ways in the Pali Canon: "as memory and as lucid awareness of present happenings" (Bodhi, 2013, p. 25) with perhaps a stronger emphasis on the latter.

While I recognize that the Buddha's use of a new definition of sati emphasizes present time awareness, I wish to use the inclusion of the older use of sati to mean "memory" in the Pali Canon to argue for the value of a traumatic return to the past in queer theory, queer meditative consciousness, and queer activism. As a result of a combination of Morrigan's (2017) work and my own deeper understanding of Buddhism and psychotherapy, I am now moving towards focusing on developing a non-attached metacognitive awareness of the time travel, an awareness of cognition, affect, and bodily sensation when past or future thoughts occur, rather than trying to avoid such thoughts or fusing with them. Part-way through the first year of my Zen priest training, which involved intensive meditation, I no longer met the diagnostic criteria for post-traumatic stress "disorder," (PTSD) which also is partially the result of extensive psychotherapy. It is also worth noting work such as Ann Cvetkovich's

(2003) deconstruction and resistance of PTSD. Cvetkovich explains that the psychiatric system created PTSD as a category in the same way that it created homosexuality as a psychiatric diagnosis. It is worth questioning why we deem reactions to trauma as "disordered". The complex trauma that I experienced is not erased, but I am no longer haunted by it against my will and can revisit the past more intentionally when doing so would be of benefit.

Queer Phenomenology and Buddhism

Sara Ahmed (2006) explains that our bodies become oriented toward things through straightening devices that shape the contours of what our consciousness allows us to love. Queers disorient sexuality and dominant notions of gender by failing to comply with cisheteronormative demands. Authoritative Buddhist texts such as the Pali, Mahayana, and Vajrayana Canons can be viewed as liturgical straightening devices that shape our consciousness into what a particular tradition considers proper Buddhist thinking; however, conflicts between these sets of authoritative texts become a source of contention over whose text or whose commentary is the most original, accurate, and transformative.

Bhikkhu Bodhi (2010) explains that whereas some Theravada Buddhists refute the authenticity of any texts beyond the Pali Canon, a phenomenon he terms "Nikaya purism" (Bodhi, 2010, n.p.), Mahayana Buddhists often belittle the *arahant* path as selfish and based on mere preliminary teachings, which Bodhi calls "Mahayana elitism" (Bodhi, 2010, n.p.). Below is a contemplation of the queer phenomenology of trauma in the queer consciousness, how this impacts queer perceptions of time, and how this relates to meditation. What follows is but one arguable perspective that, just as the earlier discussion on dualism and non-dualism, disorients the notion that there is a pan-queer phenomenological experience of time. Bodhi (1998, n.p.) argues that while the Pali canon does not explicitly discuss Mahayana conceptualizations of non-dualism, it also does not necessarily advocate for a path of dualisms. Similarly, I do not wish to argue that a non-dualistic approach is the perfect one for queer Buddhist Studies, only that it is one path of many in the context of relative and ultimate distinctions that, as Bornstein would put it, is "arguable" and may fit for some. A queer phenomenological approach disorients the notion of a pan-Buddhist perspective on all of the issues raised in this book, including the question of whether or not a queer Buddhist Studies should be oriented more towards dualism or non-dualism. I am a Zen practitioner and a non-binary person, and thus, non-dual perspectives resonate with me but may not with everyone.

Carla Freccero (2013) argues that spectral practices allow for a visiting of both the past and future that enable both mourning and hope. In her work on reparative reading, Eve Sedgwick states "hope, often a fracturing, even a traumatic thing to experience, is among the energies by which the reparatively positioned reader tries to organize the fragments and part-objects she encounters or creates" (Sedgwick, 2003, p. 146). Freccero (2013) argues that a critical practice of queer "hauntology" which allows for the influences of the spectral enhances Queer Studies. Queer spectrality describes both the ways in which queerness haunts heterosexual culture, and how queer people function as spectators to the dominant culture. Here, I wish to use queer spectrality to consider how queer consciousness is haunted by the trauma of homophobia and how queer theory is possessed by our ancestors who have passed from challenges such as suicide, AIDS-related illness, and transphobic murder. This traumatic haunting can be so painful that people may understandably attempt to use mindfulness meditation to exorcise these metaphorical ghosts, but an approach that transcends Buddhist modernism would instead allow us to develop a metacognitive awareness of this, a mindfulness of our queer minds and queer feelings.

Queer phenomenology can be applied to tonglen (compassion) meditation as well as metta (lovingkindness) meditation, in the ability of these practices to transcend the self/other dualism. In tonglen meditation, we inhale a smoke of suffering and exhale a light of compassion for ourselves and other suffering beings. When we are inhaling suffering and exhaling compassion, we can reach a point in which there is no separation between ourselves and the other person(s) for whom we are doing tonglen. The traumatizing impacts of living as a queer person in a world that systematically disadvantages us can be an opportunity to arouse a queer and trans *bodhicitta* (the awakened heart-mind) that wishes for all queer and trans people to be free from suffering and, by extension all beings to be free, including those who have harmed us.

Bodhicitta, the awakened heart-mind, is cultivated through compassion and wisdom in Mahayana Buddhism. Relative (also known as conventional) bodhicitta is the heartfelt desire to become a Buddha so that we can compassionately help others. It is based on conventional understandings of the existence of ourselves and separate beings. It involves: (1) Aspirational Bodhicitta, our intention to attain Buddhahood out of compassion for others, in which we contemplate the Four Divine Abodes (lovingkindness, compassion, equanimity, and sympathetic joy) and practice tonglen meditation; as well as (2) Engaged Bodhicitta, where we bring our desires to help others into the world while practicing the Six Paramitas (qualities to perfect) of generosity, patience, ethics, effort, meditation, and wisdom. Ultimate, also known as absolute, bodhicitta is the deep realization that there is no self to attain Buddhahood, there are no others to help, as all things are empty of a permanent, separate, self-existence. A translation of shunyata that might be easier to understand might be boundlessness rather than emptiness, because arising from a correct understanding of emptiness is the realization of the interconnectedness of all things due to their co-arising from causes and conditions.

Jun Po Denis Kelly Roshi, creator of the Emotional Koan practice says, "your angst is your liberation," (p. 4). In a queer context, we can see how our queer suffering can galvanize us towards queer bodhicitta, the desire to make the world a better place for others. Jetsunma Tenzin Palmo, a Tibetan nun who lived in a cave for 12 years and has been a champion for gender equality in Buddhism, vowed to attain Buddhahood in the female form. Inspired by her, I made a vow to attain Buddhahood in a queer form, regardless of what lifetime that happens in, because having queer Buddhist teachers means something to people, and I hope that there may be others who vow to do the same. This is a strong contrast from when I was a teenager and wished I was not queer. Queer and trans bodhicitta can be a gift that guides us on our path.

While a canonical use of sati allows us to rest in awareness of consciousness, the application of tonglen encourages us to use our own suffering for the benefit of others. The example of internalized transphobia applies here. We can observe how past trauma, alongside intergenerational trauma, that haunts a queer collective consciousness, feels incredibly painful for us, and we can embrace this suffering, breathing it in for all the other people around the world who experience this, and sending out compassion. This is similar to how, during the AIDS pandemic, people living with HIV did tonglen for all the other people in the world living with the virus, and it made them feel like there was meaning given to their experience. This was coupled with the engaged activism of groups like the AIDS Coalition to Unleash Power (ACT UP). Our queer suffering can be what deepens our queer compassion and can lead us to take action in the world to help others.

Metagenderism, Trans Deeper Knowledges, and Deity Yoga

Vajrayana Buddhism includes deity yoga practices in which the practitioner envisions themselves as the deity, regardless of their own gender, and sometimes dons clothing of the neighboring gender. An analysis of these practices using trans phenomenology and trans temporalities will bolster our discussion of transness in Buddhism. In Lama Palden Drolma's (2019) version of tonglen, the practitioner imagines themself as Kuan Yin – in her instruction Drolma describes a visualization of Kuan Yin while using "he" pronouns but notes that one can use the female form if one "prefer[s] a female" (Drolma, 2019, p. 118), not necessarily if the practitioner themself is a female. Thubten Chödrön describes in her book on the yoga method of Kuan Yin a visualization of Kuan Yin as male, stating:

Sometimes when doing deity yoga, we have a hard time imagining ourselves as a male deity if we're women, or as a female deity if we're men. It feels funny. We don't feel like "me" anymore. That shows us how much we grasp at our gender as part of our self- identity. Whereas grasping at the inherent existence of our gender is innate ignorance, developing a self-concept of what it means to be a certain gender is acquired – we learn it in this life. (Chödrön, 2005, p. 110).

Here, the "we" that Chödrön does not likely realize she is speaking to is a cisgender we, because the trans "we" may have more experience picturing ourselves as another gender than our sex assigned at birth and acquiring the mannerisms of the gender we are forced to live as, as well as the gender (or lack thereof) that we eventually get to live as when we are ready. Interestingly, deity yoga could also function as an empathy-building exercise for cisgender people, gaining a small peek into the affective feelings of dysphoria. For the trans practitioner, deity yoga could be much more uncomfortable if the sex one pictures oneself becoming is the sex assigned at birth. The notion that gender is acquired allows for a demedicalized understanding of trans identity that seizes the concept of gender dysphoria from the hands of psychiatrists who pathologize transness as a disorder.

There is precedent for an expansive view on gender in Vajrayana Buddhism. Pandaka is often translated to 'ma ning' in Tibetan, (Gyatso 2003, p.97), meaning neuter. According to Cabezón (2017, p. 443), the Ratnamālā Tantra explains that "man and woman are extremes. The neuter is nondual." A Vajrayana trans worldview allows for a spiritual non-binary epistemology that sees the nonbinary person as having a valuable spiritual attainment due to their insight into the non-dual nature of reality. Scherer (2006) explains the Tibetan Buddhist understandings of gender as a "soteriological androgyny," a salvific understanding of the non-dual transcendence of gender that calls for the practitioner to develop a spiritual state beyond binary notions of gender, a state that Scherer (2006) terms "metagenderism." This can apply to binary trans understandings as well.

Gonpo Maning Nagpo is the Tibetan translation for the name of the deity Mahakala, with the word 'maning' relating to their existence outside the gender binary (Gyatso, 2003). The gender expansive nature of this deity is honoured as part of their power: "it is because [this deity] is not definitively either male or female that [they are] able to accomplish the work of all Buddhas" (Gyatso, 2003, p. 102). Whereas Kuan Yin's gender variations are incorrectly presumed to be related to the spread of Buddhism across time and culture, Gonpo Maning Nagpo's existence outside the gender binary is indisputable and they are honoured for this among cisgender and transgender people alike. It is interesting to consider the non-binary phenomenology of Vajrayana *yidam*[6] practices in which the practitioner imagines themselves becoming Gonpo Maning Nagpo. Baker (2010, p. 362) explains that practitioners who practice the Gonpo Maning Nagpo yidam must "question, unpack and deconstruct their own sex/gender and indeed all sex/genders." Baker (2010) likens the practice to Judith Butler's (1991) notion of gender insubordination. Indeed, it may be quite a deconstructive practice or an act of gender insubordination for cisgender people to undergo, but what of the non-binary practitioner who has already done such deconstructing? Again, the practicing audience is assumed to be cisgender in Baker's (2010) work just as they are in Chödrön's (2005) book.

Non-binary people imagining themselves as Gonpo Maning Nagpo, whose existence beyond the binary is essential to their ability to accomplish the work of the Buddhas, may experience a deep validation from this practice. Gender euphoria is often discussed among Western trans people as the opposite psychological state of the medical diagnosis of gender dysphoria. Gender euphoria is a state in which a person feels joy or congruence. In Buddhist terms,

---

6 *Yidam*, meaning heart bound, is a collection of tantric practices in Vajrayana Buddhism involving working with deities to help one realize one's own Buddha nature.

gender dysphoria is often unpleasant, and euphoria is often pleasant, the former is pathologized and the latter is rarely discussed amongst the professionals who are supposed to be helping us, but is often talked about amongst community members. This affective experience is discussed solely in the corporeal context of one's own mind state in relation to how the physical body is perceived by self or others, but dominant understandings of gender euphoria may be expanded when applied to a feeling of joy that a non-binary person might experience when imagining themselves taking on the form of a gender fluid Kuan Yin or a non-binary[7] Gonpo Maning Nagpo. Buckner (2020) calls gender dysphoria a "sustained trauma" steeped in repetitive gendered remembrances and explains that Soto Zen's *shikantaza* or "just sitting" meditation along with concentrative meditations such as shamatha might exacerbate dysphoria due to its corporeal nature. It may in this case be a good opportunity to train oneself in a self-compassionate approach to dysphoria, though it is important that practitioners do not force themselves through it, and we cannot assume that any particular meditation will be difficult for all trans people, as many trans people do these meditations, but Buckner's (2020) point is well taken. Yidam practice on a trans or non-binary Buddhist deity or bodhisattva may present a euphoric alternative that can leave the practitioner feeling not only a sense of congruence and joy but also a sense of belonging as a trans person in our religion.

Practice

Rainbow Lovingkindness Meditation

Lovingkindness, also known as metta, is a Buddhist meditation that is also incorporated into mindfulness-based stress reduction. One

---

7 Here I apply the English contemporary terms 'gender fluid' and 'non-binary' for the sake of ease of flow and because of my commitment to trans visibility in Buddhist texts. See discussions in Chapters 2 and 5 that complicate and acknowledge the limits of this method.

of the goals of lovingkindness is to develop a feeling of warmth towards oneself and all beings. Metta is trained so that it can be given to anybody, regardless of how difficult of a person they might be for us. While metta is typically a formal practice, it can also be practiced informally throughout one's day, wherever we are, by repeating phrases of lovingkindness in our thoughts. This can help change our relationship to ourselves and can aid us in healing from difficulties we have had with other people.

First, ground yourself by focusing on the breath. When you are ready, visualize an image of yourself. It might be yourself sitting in front of you, it could also be an image of yourself as a child. You might visualize a warm light radiating from your heart to an image of yourself. In your mind, repeat the following phrases:

May I be safe,
May I be happy,
May I be healthy,
May I live with ease.

After repeating those phrases several times, offer lovingkindness to someone you love using the same visualization and the same phrases. You might picture them in front of you, sending a rainbow light from your heart, repeating:

May [insert name] be safe,
May they be happy,
May they be healthy,
May they live with ease.

Following this, offer lovingkindness to a stranger. It might be someone at a convenience store, or someone that you've seen walking down the street.

Once you've offered lovingkindness to a stranger, offer the phrases to someone who you struggle with. This might be someone who's wronged you. It might be helpful to remember that these phrases are really just wishing the bare minimum for that difficult person. If you find this too difficult, return to offering lovingkindness to yourself, as you too are suffering, and in need of metta.

To finish the meditation, offer lovingkindness to all beings everywhere.

Trans Bodhisattvas, Queer Practices:
Kuan Yin, Tonglen, and HIV/AIDS

Kuan Yin (also known as Avalokiteshvara or Chenrezig, depending on the language and tradition) is a bodhisattva who has been revered by queer and trans people as a queer being. One of the most beautiful stories of Kuan Yin comes through their depiction with one-thousand arms and eleven heads. In this story, Kuan Yin vowed to never rest until all beings were free of suffering; however, despite all efforts, they still had not attained their goal. They expended such tireless efforts to comprehend the suffering of all beings that their head split into eleven pieces. Amitabha Buddha saw their efforts and granted them eleven heads to hear the cries of everyone in the world. After hearing the world's cries, they tried to reach out to all the beings in the world when suddenly their arms fell off and broke into pieces. They were then granted one thousand arms by Amitabha Buddha so that they could help as many beings as possible. This is one of many stories of the bodhisattva's great compassion. The diverse depictions of their genders that follow may also be a by-product of their compassionate wish to aid the suffering of all beings, including queer people.

Cathryn Bailey (2009) explains that Kuan Yin is depicted across many cultures, traditions, and countries as male, female, both, and neither. In the *Lotus Sutra*, the Buddha is asked, "World-Honored One, why does Regarder of the Cries of the World Bodhisattva [Kuan Yin] travel around in this world? How does he teach the Dharma for the sake of the living? What sort of power of skillful means does he have?" (Reeves, 2008, p. 373). The Buddha responds with lists of ways in which Kuan Yin can change form in order to help those in need. The Buddha states: "for those who need someone in the body of a boy or girl in order to be saved, he appears as a boy or girl and teaches the Dharma for them" (Reeves, 2008, p. 374).

If I may once again dare to travel the dangerous terrain of personal narrative, humanizing this work, I will share that earlier in graduate school, I was a foster parent for queer and trans youth. One of my trans foster children had Buddhist birth parents. They called Kuan Yin "gender fluid," which is specifically a sub-category of non-binary identity that I actually ended up embracing for myself later on. Our earlier discussion of anachronisms can be applied here to consider how the application of this contemporary English language term can allow us to combat the erasure of trans communities in Buddhist cosmology. Even if the issue of history were not at play, Kuan Yin's influence spans across many different cultures and countries and thus refuses attempts to locate a geographic, culturally, and linguistically appropriate gender expansive identity. My use of the term 'gender fluid' is an attempt to make legible that part of Kuan Yin's story which is often illegible to cisgender, heterosexual eyes – eyes that dispossess us of any hold we have on the existence of people or bodhisattvas like us. I recognize the flaws in this approach and proceed with the conviction that the benefits of my intentions remain. I use my foster son's choice of 'gender fluid' over terms such as 'non-binary' because it adequately captures the *Lotus Sutra*'s depiction of Kuan Yin as changing genders according to the needs of the person they are helping.

Cathryn Bailey (2009) explains that while some claim Kuan Yin was originally depicted as a male figure in India in the beginning of the Common Era and then subsequently as female by the 12th century in China and Japan, it remains inaccurate to assume that this is due to some imagined (and rather Orientalist) assumption of regional gendered associations with compassion. She complicates the assumption that Kuan Yin was depicted as female due to an association of compassion with the feminine by explaining that some might argue that in China, compassion was, if anything, historically more of a masculinized quality (Bailey, 2009). She explains that Kuan Yin is still often depicted as male and as androgynous in a variety of countries, and it is therefore inaccurate to claim that the bodhisattva "used to be" male and is now female (Bailey, 2009). In fact, in some temples there may be multiple artworks of this bodhisattva displayed, with Kuan Yin depicted in a different gender in each piece. Bailey (2009) asserts that Kuan Yin embodies a pragmatic approach to the feminist question of gender essentialism as we can use their story to examine gender through the lens of non-Self due to its changing nature.

Queer Trauma and Queer Community Post-Traumatic Growth

As a marginalized group, queers are strongly attuned to the overwhelming suffering that occurs in this world; indeed, part of living as queer is the affective work of compassion for the pain of others in our communities. Some queer people even develop compassion for our tormentors. Eve Sedgwick, a cisgender, heterosexual queer theorist who also writes on Buddhism, begins her book *Tendencies* by stating "I think everyone who does gay and lesbian studies is haunted by the suicides of adolescents," (Sedgwick, 1993, p. 1) as a way of honoring how our pens are metaphorically possessed by the ghosts of queer and trans ancestors as we write about our suffering in Queer Studies. After seeing many queer people around me die by suicide, this metaphorical haunting is what led me to do my doctoral dissertation on how AIDS activist approaches could help us develop an approach to queer suicide prevention that involves structural activism. There are myriad other examples of queer suffering, such as murder, the death penalty in many countries, government inaction on AIDS, attacks on trans healthcare, and the outcasting of queer people from our families. The magnitude of queer suffering is such that, in these painful times, a theorization of queer necropolitics has been conceptualized to describe the power to inequitably distribute death amongst certain multiply marginalized queers in juxtaposition to the more privileged queers who are afforded acceptance through assimilation. Achilles Mbembé (2003, p. 40) coined the term 'necropolitics' as a way to describe "death-worlds, new and unique forms of social existence in which vast populations are subjected to conditions of life conferring upon them the status of living dead." Jasbir Puar conceptualized queer necropolitics as a way of understanding how certain, more privileged queer people are, in her words, "folded into life" (Puar, 2017, p. 36), allowed a higher chance at survival due to their assimilability, while others inhabiting multiple marginalized identities are exposed to greater rates of premature death. There is an affective component of queer necropolitics, and necropolitical times broadly, that remains largely unexplored in the literature. It is my contention is that these traumatic times are ripe for the development of queer bodhicitta, the queer awakened heart-mind, which I connect to the rather queer practice of tonglen in what follows.

Ann Cvetkovich's (2003) work on queer trauma as omnipresent is helpful in this discussion of queer suffering. Cvetkovich (2003) develops her notion of queer trauma counter to the medicalized discourse of post-traumatic stress disorder through her exploration of lesbian AIDS activism and her discussion of the often daily painful experiences that queers have to live through. Cvetkovich (2003) ultimately argues that queer suffering has led to the formation of queer trauma cultures, communities informed by trauma that are imbued with elements of caring, mourning, activism, and compassion – concepts crucial to a queer engaged Buddhism.

I join Heather Love (2009) in her rather Buddhist argument that we need a study of queer affect that embraces rather than runs away from difficult feelings and I argue that we must extend the queer study of queer affect into the surprisingly under-researched affect of queer compassion. Just as the Buddha began his spiritual path after bearing witness to the suffering of old age, sickness, and death, queers are particularly attuned to suffering and thus a queer compassion can be readily engaged. Queer suffering in necropolitical times is not only painful; it has also led to a form of community post-traumatic growth. Positive psychology researchers noticed profound changes in folks after trauma and documented these to counter the sole focus on psychopathology. Post-traumatic growth often involves an "increased appreciation for life in general, more meaningful interpersonal relationships, an increased sense of personal strength, changed priorities, and a richer existential and spiritual life" (Tedeschi & Calhoun, 2004, p. 1). In Muncaster (2023),

I explore what I call "queer community post-traumatic growth," expanding this to queer folks as a group, who have gained incredible tools for care and activism due to the challenges our communities have been through. This post-traumatic growth manifests through the affective and political arousal of queer bodhicitta, the compassionate awakening of a heart-mind aspiration to alleviate the suffering of all beings, which Pema Chödrön (2001) explains is the foundation of tonglen practice.

Rainbow Tonglen Compassion Meditation, Political Depression, and Queer Feelings

Tonglen meditation, also known as "sending and taking" and "exchanging self for others" is a Vajrayana practice that is both queer in its counterintuitive instruction and has philosophical as well as practical implications for the development of a queer engaged Buddhism. Tonglen is the seventh instruction in the fifty-nine Tibetan *lojong* slogans (mind training practices used to enhance one's compassion) which states "...sending and taking should be practiced alternately. These two should ride the breath" (Chödrön, 2001, p. 33). In a popular version, the meditator arouses bodhicitta and breathes in a smoke that is the suffering of the person or people whom they want to work with in the meditation (which can include oneself) and breathes out a bright light that represents compassion and the wish that these beings be free from that suffering (Chödrön, 2007). When I taught tonglen as part of Rainbodhi's *Compassionate Queers* online workshop series, I suggested that practitioners consider doing this for a queer person they know who is in pain, all queers, themselves, or for a case of internalized homophobia, and to consider breathing out a rainbow light to represent tapping into their queer potentiality for compassion (Muncaster, 2021a, n.p.).[8] Because it is quite common for students to report

---

8 See this video for the session: https://www.youtube.com/watch?v=MPZnUCQdqIc&t=775s

the practice as emotionally difficult, Lama Palden Drolma (2019, p. 21) developed a more digestible version which she calls "love on every breath" where, rather than absorbing the suffering into oneself, a practitioner imagines themselves taking on the form of the aforementioned queer-coded Kuan Yin and then does tonglen as the bodhisattva of compassion.

Tonglen's queer instruction is counter-intuitive when juxtaposed to dualistic New Age meditations that ask the practitioner to inhale the positive and exhale the negative. This practice also implies a critique of the Western, individualistic notion of self-care, which fails to consider the importance of care for one's community. Tonglen combats this through its transcendence of the self/other distinction. The eleventh of *The Thirty-Seven Practices of a Bodhisattva* by Tokme Zongpo states:

> All suffering, without exception, arises from the desire
>   for one's own happiness.
> Perfect buddhas are born from benefiting others.
> Therefore, to perfectly exchange one's own happiness
> For others' suffering is the practice of a bodhisattva.
>   (Norbu, 2020, p. 4).

This verse touches on the concept of non-duality, the notion that there is no separation between the pain experienced by the self and that of another. Those on the bodhisattva path cannot fathom liberation until all are freed from suffering. In context of activism, intersectional feminist analysis allows us to see oppressions as mutually reinforcing, thus, queer liberation struggles will not succeed without addressing other forms of marginalization. In their chapter in *Transcending: Trans Buddhist Voices*, Finn Enke (2019) implores us to stop trying to figure out if Kuan Yin is "really" male or female and instead engage in the more productive work of seeing Kuan Yin as the embodiment of non-duality.

We can use the eleventh stanza of *The Thirty-Seven Practices of a Bodhisattva* to expand queer writing on (un)happiness. Sara Ahmed's work on unhappy queers problematizes the heteronormative imperative for individuals to spend life seeking happiness in narrowly defined forms, explaining, "queers can be affectively alien by placing their hopes for happiness in the wrong objects, as well as being made unhappy by conventional routes of happiness, an unhappiness which might be an effect of how your happiness makes others unhappy" (Ahmed, 2010, p. 115). Unhappiness itself can be political, as we see in Ann Cvetkovich's (2012) work exploring Feel Tank Chicago's notion of political depression, coined by activists who sought to make public the privatized feelings of discontent with structural inequities such as capitalism. Feel Tank Chicago held protests where activists showed up in bathrobes with signs with slogans such as "Depressed? It might be political!" to highlight how often our suffering is rooted in structures such as capitalism, queerphobia, sexism, and racism.

Since the second of the Buddhist three marks of existence is suffering, it behooves a queer Buddhist politic to turn toward, rather than away from the ways in which oppression makes queers unhappy. The eleventh stanza explains that our suffering stems from our desire for our own happiness and implores us to exchange our happiness for the suffering of others. We can put Ahmed's (2010) work in conversation with this verse by asking the question, as if it is a Zen koan: is it possible or desirable for queers to maintain happiness or to feign a gratitude for what little we have when other queer people are suffering? Much resentment has built in queer communities over the more privileged queers divesting themselves from activism and community work once their aims have been achieved, for example, gay marriage, and leaving others suffering under different challenges such as administrative violence against trans people, with little help.

In a talk hosted virtually by Rainbodhi, Lama Rod Owens, known for his book *Love and Rage: The path of liberation through anger* (Owens, 2020), explained that the bodhisattva is an expression of queerness. He argued that the bodhisattva concept is queer because it must maintain a fluidity in order to disrupt the roots of violence and that bodhisattvas are sassy in their activism. In addition to allowing for difficult emotions in the face of queer struggle, we can feel sympathetic joy for the queer success of others. Owens explained that by demonstrating our own joy and outwardly existing, we enable other queers who see us to experience their own queer joy. It reminds me of the cognitive dissonance I feel around holding hands with men. I really like holding hands, I feel loved when I hold hands. I also feel hypervigilant, scanning my environment as I sometimes wonder if I and the other person will be physically harmed. Sometimes, the motivation of knowing that it means something to other queer strangers passing by to see me holding hands gives me the determination to keep holding hands and not give in to the temptation to let go. Owens explained that one element of the bodhisattva path can be living our authentic queer lives (if we are in a safe place to do so) because it is liberating for other queer people to see us choosing to exist.

In the face of an overwhelming amount of queer suffering in these necropolitical times, queers have engaged in tireless activism to ameliorate the systemic roots of our oppression. This queer resilience resonates with stanza eighteen of *The Thirty-Seven Practices of a Bodhisattva*:

> Even when I am made destitute, people constantly
>   berate me,
> And grave illness and evil spirits strike me,
> To take on still the suffering and misdeeds of all beings
>   for myself
> Without losing heart is the practice of a bodhisattva.
> (Norbu, 2020, p. 5)

While the intention of this stanza may be to encourage the practice of tonglen even in the most difficult of circumstances, we can press pause on the meditation piece for a moment and consider how queers have long been following the instructions of stanza eighteen through the caring communities of queer trauma cultures and through activism. When mass deaths occurred during the height of the still on-going AIDS pandemic, queers were devastated by an overwhelming amount of grief. Not losing heart, as stanza eighteen recommends, queers demonstrated activist resistance and resilience through groups such as the AIDS Coalition to Unleash Power (ACT UP) that engaged in tireless direct-action efforts to demand government action on AIDS (Cvetkovich, 2003, p. 10). Some queer people find forgiveness to be important to their healing and have let go of resentment for incredible suffering.

Anti-queer hate and health: HIV/AIDS, COVID-19, and Mpox

I have worked in the severely underfunded frontline HIV/AIDS social services sector in Canada and in biomedical HIV research for much of my career, but I have lived with the trauma of the pandemic since I came out as queer. That moment when my mother screamed at me that because I was gay I was going to give her AIDS through a towel, she instilled a fear that haunted my sexual encounters for years to come (Muncaster, 2021b), until I eventually learned more about how the virus actually works. Coming from one of two pandemics that is on-going, it has been difficult to watch as forces mobilized and our world changed to help slow the COVID-19 pandemic (referred to in popular discourse as "the" pandemic by those who may believe that AIDS is over) because it impacted people who matter, the general population, rather than queers and other marginalized groups, the elimination of whom would delight many homophobic and transphobic people. I continued this work of practicing stanza eighteen of *The Thirty-Seven Practices of a Bodhisattva*, trying not to lose heart while I watched queers and Black communities get blamed for the 2022 monkeypox outbreak, a disease which the World Health Organization renamed to Mpox to reduce anti-Black racism. I continue to try not to lose heart while reading comments such as one I read on a YouTube video of Canadian news on monkeypox (Global News, 2022) that stated: "The alphabet community, again giving us more of what we don't want.... After their month long [Pride] celebration what did the 'experts' think was going to happen!"[9] I have also been told by a homophobe there are not enough jails to hold queers and that we should be put in camps to protect heterosexual people and their children from Mpox, nearly identical language to that used in AIDS pandemic. Vaccine hoarding in the Global North prevented countries in the Global South from having access to the smallpox vaccine (which can prevent Mpox and reduce symptom severity and death), which would have prevented this outbreak to begin with. Canada had these vaccines stored in freezers for years in case there was another smallpox outbreak and released them during the Mpox outbreak. It was not until the pandemic had already changed the lives of so many queer people and after the work of mass queer-led protests, before many world leaders, including presidents and prime ministers, even said the words "HIV/AIDS" publicly or even its prior name which was Gay-Related Immune Disease (GRID). My Buddhist practice helps; I am trying so hard, as a queer person living in this world, not to lose heart. I ran one of the vaccine clinics and luckily the outbreak improved dramatically in Canada, but we must consider how marginalized groups continue to be scapegoats blamed for health issues and we must remember the importance of international solidarity. I conducted a survey on stigma with patients at the Mpox vaccine clinic where I worked in Toronto, and many of the patients worried about media and public discourse which blamed queer people for the outbreak (Muncaster et al., 2024).

Jackson (1995) describes the impact of AIDS as well as reformist and modernist Buddhist thought on queer communities in Thailand. He discusses two opposing views on homosexuality: the traditional view which sees homosexuality as attributable to past karma and thus outside the control of the individual, and the reformist view that homosexuality is the product of an individual's previously immoral acts in either a past life or one's

---

9 Commented publicly by YouTube user Korky on https://www.youtube.com/watch?v=GiSRxy5sSjo

current life. The former, more sympathetic, though also problematic, view sees homosexuality, transness, and intersexuality as congenital conditions that cannot be altered in one's current life. In this view, queerness, transness, and intersexuality do not cause negative consequences in future lives. The latter view sees homosexuality as a willful violation of what is seen as so-called "natural" heterosexual conduct and is emblematic of the violator's lack of self-control. Jackson explains that reformist and modernist understandings of Buddhism are often seen as progressive due to their opposition of the historical alignment of the sangha with the state and the military; whereas metaphysical views of Buddhism that emphasize karma are seen as backward and conservative. Despite this, it is this seemingly progressive interpretation of Buddhism that has a more harmful impact on queer people.

AIDS was seen as punishment for gay sex (as some Christians also saw it), with the "vaccine" being the Buddhist practice of *kayagatasati*, or observing the unpleasantness and unsatisfactoriness of the body, among gay people. Such meditative practices are intended to make the person disgusted with sex by imagining the various organs and bodily fluids that make up the human body. This misuse of kayagatasati is essentially meditative conversion therapy. I am hesitant to even describe it here for fear that folks with internalized queerphobia might try the "practice" and if you are reading this and feel tempted to do kayagatasati for conversion therapy purposes, please reach out to someone for support instead. Some Buddhist scriptures caution that this meditative practice does not always have its intended effect. Jackson (1995) describes scriptures in which some monks went to charnel grounds and graveyards to contemplate the decaying nature of the body and ended up practicing necrophilia. He also explains that the Buddha urged caution in this practice in another instance when some monks died by suicide because they become so repulsed with their own bodies. Indeed, Blosnich and colleagues (2020) explain that conversion therapy leads to dramatic increases in suicide among queer people.

Jackson (1995) notes that there were also changes in understandings of the kathoey in Thailand from being defined by a so-called 'gender imbalance' to then being defined more by their sexuality. This conflation is similar to the 'gender inversion' concept that was at one time dominant in the West as well. Jackson discusses how the pandaka was seen as a precursor to the kathoey. He also explains that the abhorrent narratives around homosexuality during the AIDS pandemic actually served to consolidate notions of gay identity in Thailand. The same has been said of the AIDS pandemic in other parts of the world and its ties to queer and trans activism.

Sex workers have been subjected to whorephobic discourse blaming them for the AIDS pandemic and seeing them as vectors of disease. Sex workers are often actually ambassadors for sexual health in their communities, teaching clients and each other advanced sexual health knowledge. There is lore that sees Kuan Yin as a sex worker and Goddess of sex workers. We see this reflected in the poem below that uses the outdated word 'prostitute':

Kuan Yin / The Prostitute

She is passion and no passion
    she is not separate from me
    a projection of energy
of form, of emptiness
    movements of things
    may or may not exist
I am Kuan Yin/the prostitute
    breathing together one breath
    a whirling Shiva within the space of mind
    imprints of a bird in sky
    Kuan Yin/the prostitute different
    yet the same
Love the prostitute in me
    as well as Kuan Yin
    darkness as well as light
    Kuan Yin holds her arms
    around the prostitute

the prostitute holds her arms
around Kuan Yin
Kuan Yin's lips bright red
no lips at all
prostitute/Kuan Yin did it to me
it was done
the opening,
lipstick on the wind, bright red.
                    (Pat Donegan, cited in Boucher, 2000, p. 106)

Many of the problematic narratives around sex work and HIV do not take into account the fact that the reason sex workers are at a higher risk for HIV acquisition is largely due to workplace violence that is enabled by anti-sex work laws that make it difficult to negotiate boundaries before an encounter (for example, in Canada at the time of writing, soliciting in public is illegal) and make it difficult to call for help if an issue arises. Seeing a positive reflection of sex work embodied in a bodhisattva can mean a lot to a community that is treated so poorly.

Pema Chödrön (2016) explains how tonglen was used amongst people dying of AIDS-related complications during the height of the AIDS pandemic. She discusses how people living with HIV would breathe in the suffering of all the other people around the world who had the virus and breathe out compassion. She quoted a man who told her, "…it doesn't hurt me. It makes me feel that my pain is not in vain, that I am not alone and useless. It makes all of this worthwhile" (Chödrön, 2016, p. 90). Even while dying, queer people have held onto a compassionate drive to help others.

I attended a hybrid online and in-person retreat with Pema Chödrön on tonglen, hosted by the Omega Institute in 2022, her last retreat with the organization. There was a question from the in-person audience from a queer man who grew up in the 1980s and felt that the AIDS activist organization ACT UP was born of rage. He felt that there was no time to lose, that there was an impulsivity to act now in order to stop the deaths due to government inaction. Chödrön noted that she would have to think about that because

it was difficult for her to imagine aggression bringing down bar-
riers. She did note that anger was not a bad thing in her eyes, but
we must befriend it. The next day she returned to the question after having done some research on ACT UP. She admired the non-
violence of ACT UP. She said that there was a time in which tonglen
was taught in AIDS hospices and during this time she received a lot
of letters from people living with HIV who were doing the practice.
One man said that the symptoms of the syndrome were not as bad
for him as the emotional states of shame, self-disgust, hopeless-
ness, and despair that he felt, and that when he was taught tonglen,
for the first time his disease had meaning now because he was doing it for all the other people who had HIV / AIDS. He did tonglen
not just for the symptoms but for these difficult emotions that he
knew from talking to others were so widespread. We can also look
to Maitri hospice developed by Issan Dorsey who was an HIV positive Zen Roshi, queer person, drag queen, sex worker, and person
who struggled with drugs. Dorsey used the rooms in a Zen temple
in San Francisco to house people dying of AIDS-related illnesses
(Schneider, 2020, p. 177). For affluent people in the Global North,
HIV has become more of a chronic illness, but the situation is very
different in the Global South. I have seen the benefit of tonglen both
as a practice and an attitude in my professional life as a therapist
and it has deeply impacted my personal life.

Stories of Kuan Yin and the practice and philosophy behind
tonglen meditation have much to offer queer activism. Sedgwick
(2003) explains that part of the pedagogy of Buddhism lies in its
simultaneous emphasis on experiential learning and its delineation
between cognitive ways of knowing and the affective and corporeal realization of truths. During these queer necropolitical times,
queers are engaged in extensive compassionate activism. There is
a pedagogical value in Buddhist stories of Kuan Yin and in tonglen
meditation as we can understand that compassion is not solely an
emotion, it is an affective and tangible practice that must be honed
throughout a lifetime. Compassion is action. This allows us to understand compassion through a lens that is limitless, boundless,
and inherently queer, not only due to Kuan Yin's gender fluidity

but also because of its counterintuitive (to the Western imaginary) exhortation that we completely exchange the conventional self for others. It is a practice that involves forgoing individualism, which is a mindset that is a luxury not often afforded to marginalized groups.

It is not my intention with this chapter to argue that all queers must worship Kuan Yin and practice tonglen, though I admit my own disposition towards seeing the benefits of these practices for socially engaged Buddhism. Rather, it is compassion as praxis that undergirds this work. I hope to spark a larger conversation on the affective politics of what Owens (2021, n.p.) terms 'the queer bodhisattva,' which inspired me to write this book, and to unearth how compassion as praxis can benefit both engaged Buddhism and Queer Studies. The sheer volume of Buddhist thought on compassion can contribute immensely to queer activism, which has, since its inception, been steeped in compassionate praxis. What I term 'queer engaged Buddhism' expands on existing engaged Buddhist literature which continually leaves out explicit engagement with queerness. Such an approach should consider compassion as praxis as quintessential to an activism that is intersectional, fluid, and recognizes the mutually reinforcing nature of oppressions.

Practice

Rainbow Tonglen Compassion Meditation

There is a great deal of suffering in queer communities which offers opportunities for deepening our compassion.

Tonglen, the practice of sending and taking is a compassion meditation practiced in many forms of Buddhism but largely in the Vajrayana tradition.

Here, we inhale suffering and exhale compassion, a bit counterintuitive to the new age meditations of inhaling the good and exhaling the bad. We want to learn not to turn away from suffering.

Atisha, an Indian Buddhist teacher who introduced the 59 mind training, or lojong, slogans in his work in Tibet has a slogan, or mind training instruction, about tonglen: Lojong 7. Sending and taking should be practiced alternately. These two should ride the breath.

Sometimes we get triggered and this meditation allows us to gently expose ourselves to pain and be able to move through it. We can learn from the triggers, just trying not to go too deep too fast, we can pick an issue of mild intensity. We're not necessarily actually taking in the person's suffering through an imagined energy; we're trying to open our hearts. Nothing bad is going to happen to us.

Shantideva, an Indian Buddhist monk highly influential in Tibetan Buddhism explains that we need to transcend the social construction of self/other, which mirrors our queer assertion of transcending constructed binaries. Tokme Zongpo puts this beautifully in stanza eleven of *The Thirty-Seven Practices of a Bodhisattva*:

> All suffering comes from the wish for your own
>   happiness.
> Perfect Buddhas are born from the thought to help
>   others.
> Therefore exchange your own happiness
>   for the suffering of others –
> This is the practice of Bodhisattvas.

Tonglen has been one of the most powerful practices in my life. I find it gives me the tools to encounter pain I feel and to enhance my compassion for others. Here are the steps:

Grounding through the breath, perhaps beginning by relaxing the body.

Resting in awakened heart-mind (what Pema Chödrön calls a flash of bodhichitta). Bodhicitta is the aspiration to help all beings and also the action of taking a stand in social justice. It is insight into the nature of suffering and compassion in our world. Imagining our heart expanding and really conjuring up that motivation to be there for oneself and all beings.

Visualization: Inhaling a smoke of suffering (any colour, or you can personify it as a snake or a being), exhaling a rainbow of compassion from the heart-center.

Thinking of a personal situation, something you're struggling with, not starting with a trauma. If you'd like to relate it to queerness you can think about an issue of internalized queerphobia, something about being queer that you find challenging, or a challenge you've had with someone, but not the worst thing. Inhaling for yourself and exhaling compassion. Then doing this for other queer people in a similar circumstance as you. If you are struggling, either a) imagine yourself as Kuan Yin or another compassionate being who is taking in this suffering and exhaling compassion or b) do tonglen for yourself and all people currently struggling with the meditation.

You can then expand it to a queer person you love, a neutral person, someone you might be upset with, all queer people, and then all beings.

6

Buddhist Psychotherapy and Spiritual Care for Queer and Trans Communities

When I was putting together the course called Buddhism and Psychotherapy, for the Buddhism, Psychology, and Mental Health program at the University of Toronto: New College, I was baffled to discover that Buddhism either influenced or could be strongly connected to nearly every therapy that I could think to put on the syllabus. I went through all of the Western forms of psychotherapy that I could remember and searched for articles that discussed a relationship of these methods to Buddhism. Of course, I expected all the mindfulness-based psychotherapies to be influenced by Buddhism, but I was surprised to hear that thinkers behind other therapies such as Gestalt therapy had studied Buddhist literature.

This demonstrated to me how strongly Buddhism has influenced Western psychotherapy, beyond just the mindfulness movement. At the same time, it is important that we consider the Buddhist modernist (McMahan, 2008) time period we live in, a time in which the esoteric parts of Buddhism are eschewed for concepts such as mindfulness meditation that fit within the so-called "rational," scientific model. This rational/emotional divide is rooted in sexism. I call Buddhist modernism a temporality rather than a set of acts because it coalesces with concepts in the contemporary world such as the age of enlightenment, globalization, and Orientalism. How do we justify the incorporation of Buddhist techniques in Western psychotherapy while avoiding cultural appropriation? I found some solace in Bhikkhu Bodhi's (2013) work where he explains that ultimately, the Buddhist teachings were meant to end suffering and thus, if mindfulness helps people, that is great; however, as Buddhists, we would prefer that people consider learning more about where these practices come from and that they look into other aspects of the Eightfold Path beyond just meditation.

Bhikkhu Anālayo (2020) combats the argument that the popular eight-week mindfulness training program, Mindfulness-Based Stress Reduction (MBSR), is a form of McMindfulness, making people subservient to neoliberal capitalism through learning self-regulation rather than engaging in political action (2020). He explains that mindfulness does not mean the absence of thought and therefore does not necessarily depoliticize people, who are still agents of their own lives, and is line with Buddhist teachings. He makes an interesting point regarding individual autonomy, and I would also suggest that we must still resist difficult structures in addition to coping with them. He argues in Anālayo (2022) that the critique of Buddhist modernism might have become so exaggerated that it has tipped the scales of Buddhist discourse in a manner that is not accurate to Buddhist teachings, asserting that works such as Donald Lopez's (2009) book on Buddhism and science involve misunderstandings of Buddhist teachings. Thompson (2020) argues that it is wrong to think that Buddhism is a psychology based on meditation. Anālayo uses the Pali texts to explain that Buddhism is exactly that. Buddhist realizations about the mind are a part of observation through the direct experience of meditation and Anālayo argues that it is not Orientalism to honour the value of that. Anālayo explains that claims that it is Buddhist exceptionalism to see a relationship between Buddhism and science are overexaggerated, based on a lack of knowledge of Buddhism, and demonstrate the limits of the Buddhist modernist critique, which, while very valuable and important, in Anālayo's eyes can be overgeneralized. Anālayo (2019) explains:

> It [is] important to acknowledge that psychology and Buddhist meditation are different knowledge systems with distinct epistemologies and dissimilar final aims. Nevertheless, they converge on a keen interest in understanding the workings of the mind with a view to alleviate unnecessary suffering. This common ground can become an arena for an open dialogue that avoids

both a quest for validation and an attempt to trump the other. (Anālayo 2019, p. 13).

I do not profess to know what the right answer is. I see a lot of value in the Buddhist modernist critique regarding how problematic it is that the mindfulness movement has turned into a capitalist industry and how much of Buddhist teachings have been drained of any spiritual elements that seem incompatible with Western thought so as to be more appealing to Westerners. As well, I see how Buddhism has perhaps the most comprehensive understanding of psychology in the world and how, as Bhikkhu Bodhi (2013) notes, the point has always been to help suffering beings. I ask the reader to contemplate, as if it is a koan: how can we respectfully engage Buddhist and Western psychologies?

Therapeutic Encounters

I discovered meditation when I went into foster care, from two incredible feminist women, one a teacher and one a psychotherapist, who were both interested in the mindfulness movement. My sociology teacher in high school let me copy some of her Jon Kabat-Zinn CDs and the psychotherapist introduced me to Christopher Germer's work on self-compassion. The psychotherapist taught me the R.A.I.N. meditation for difficult emotions. The acronym stands for Recognize, Allow, Investigate, and Nourish with Self-Compassion, and a version of that meditation is in this book. My therapist at the time described self-compassion as emancipating because now we are empowered to comfort ourselves during difficult times when others may not be around. As I began a journey of learning how to label and understand the emotions that I experienced, she told me that at any time, she could list three things that she was feeling. This baffled me. I sometimes could not list even one, and it had not occurred to me that a person could experience multiple emotions at the same time. Now, when I introduce these concepts to my counselling clients, students, and friends, I am able to say the same thing my therapist said, that I am generally able to list multiple feelings that I am experiencing at any given time. When I got to the first year of my undergraduate degree, a professor who worked in equine therapy said, "emotions do not happen to us, they happen for us," and I tried to embody this rather Buddhist understanding of turning towards difficult emotions (I prefer the term "difficult" to "negative" emotions) rather than running from our suffering. These early experiences of meditation made me curious about Buddhism as a religion. Like many Westerners, psychology was my gateway to Buddhism; I wanted to be able to honour the roots of where these practices came from.

Later in my adulthood, I developed what I and some researchers (Cohen et al., 2002) call post-traumatic fibromyalgia syndrome (PTFS) (Muncaster, 2023), a chronic pain disease. Approximately half of people with this fibromyalgia syndrome also meet the diagnostic criteria for post-traumatic stress disorder (PTSD). (Cohen et al., 2002) Queer author Mattilda Bernstein Sycamore (2006) explains that "fibromyalgia is a word for this relentless cycle of pain and exhaustion that is the physical manifestation of my struggles to survive what happened in the house where I grew up, and that still resides in my body, in my brain, *in these poor hands that never could have protected me*" (Sycamore, 2010, p. 14, cited in Muncaster, 2023). As someone whose hands could not protect them from childhood violence, this explanation of the syndrome resonated deeply. Another queer writer, Leah Lakshmi Piepzna-Samarasinha similarly locates their fibromyalgia in trauma:

> …a childhood filled with abuse, terror, and a need to sleep as much as possible [that] bleeds into chronically tired yet overachieving college years, bleeds into the early twenties when I walked back into my incest memories, got sick, and spent a lot of time on my futon, struggling with fatigue, pain, and shakiness (Piepzna-Samarasinha, 2006, p. 180-181, cited in Muncaster, 2023).

These, along with Lady Gaga's experience of fibromyalgia and PTSD (Hawa, 2018, cited in Muncaster, 2023), led me to realize that I was among a community of queer people whose trauma impacted the body. I began seeing a gay Buddhist psychotherapist who felt that my fibromyalgia had traumatic origins. This does not mean that every case of fibromyalgia comes from trauma – though it appears that approximately half do (Cohen et al., 2002).

This highlights the importance of embodied practices for healing trauma, which I found largely through yoga, voguing, and martial arts, as difficult as sometimes they are to do with my condition. Yoga gave me immense peace, quieting a mind filled with anxious thoughts. Voguing allowed me to reclaim those parts of myself that I pushed away. My voguing instructors would tell me "You need to be more gay in your movements," and "just fag out," celebrating movements that I used to be bullied for, like the broken wrist. José Muñoz (2019) discusses the power of queer gesture. He talks about how he would try to butch up after seeing men walk more stiffly. He discusses his fascination upon seeing Kevin Aviance vogue and he explores voguing as both a celebration of queerness but also as a resilient act of queer and racialized survival. Martial arts made me feel safer after having experienced a life of violence. While sparring was at times triggering, it also acted as a form of exposure therapy in a safer, spiritual place.

I began seeing a gay Buddhist psychiatrist (different from the psychotherapist) who helped me explore medication options for the various difficulties I experienced. I bring this here because many people in spiritual communities may be hesitant about medication. I see this hesitation in my counselling clients as well as in my community. I assigned Mark Epstein's (2008) work when I taught Buddhism and Psychotherapy to address the issue. Mindfulness, psychotherapy, and psychopharmaceuticals are often positioned as a panacea cure-for-all, when in reality, each of these things may not work for everyone. Epstein explains that some Buddhists may hesitate to take psychopharmaceuticals, feeling that their Buddhist practice should suffice, but there is no such prohibition in Buddhism. Eventually, as my practice grew stronger, I was able to wean off of them; though, some folks may benefit from medications longer term.

Buddhist Approaches to Grief

I volunteer as a Grief Counsellor for the Toronto Centre for Applied Buddhism. When former psychotherapist and now Buddhist nun, Venerable Bhikkuni Thích Nữ Tịnh Quang, trained me in grief counselling, she taught some valuable exercises that I ended up using in both my own life as well as with my clients. I had heard of the exercise in which you write a letter to someone and you do not send it. Bhikkhuni Tịnh Quang added another layer to this. She suggested that after the original letter is written, you pretend to be the other person and you write back, completing the conversation. I asked her: what if the other person is very harsh and you end up writing yourself a hurtful letter from their point of view? She said, in her experience, most of the letters written back come from an understanding point of view. I did the exercise and the letter I "received" was relatively cordial. I've had clients ask me the same question. Some did the exercise and, while the letter they received was not so friendly, it was not as mean-spirited as they expected, and it was still very helpful for their grieving process. I find the exercise, due to its dialoguing nature, provides a level of closure that is not always possible for people due to the death of a person or perhaps because actually talking to the person (in abusive situations, for example) would be unhelpful. She also taught a Buddhist Gestalt empty chair technique that we can do when we are stuck. We can sit in a chair and express what we are feeling. Then we can put the Buddha in a chair, sit in that chair, and respond to ourselves as if we are him.

I went through my own grief counselling, which I discuss in Muncaster (2021b), through the AIDS Bereavement and Resiliency Program of Ontario (ABRPO). When I worked in frontline HIV/AIDS, we attended grief retreats each year. Even though, for the privileged with access to medication, HIV is no longer a death sentence and is instead a chronic illness that does not shorten the lifespan, ABRPO continued and workers processed grief from their personal lives as well as from the opioid epidemic, which our organization battled by creating a safe consumption site. When the group facilitators introduced themselves, there was mention of some influence from Buddhism. Workers who needed more support were provided with individual grief counselling. My counsellor and I went through a tool that I now use with a lot of my clients, called the Multiple Loss Journey. (Perreault, Fitton, & McGovern, 2010) My counsellor was an older, HIV positive man, who used to work at the AIDS Committee of Toronto during the height of the AIDS crisis. During that time, 100 of their clients died within the span of a year. The community realized that dominant approaches to the stages of grief may apply to those who have experienced a single loss but were not necessarily the same for those who have experienced multiple losses; thus, the Multiple Loss Journey, a non-linear map, was created. So many queer people experience multiple losses: losing families, communities, careers, partners, and losing a sense of safety. The Multiple Loss Journey helped me normalize the immense suffering that I had experienced and became highly relevant for my clients.

A colleague of mine in HIV used to host weekly Buddhist harm reduction groups. Community members appreciated the harm reduction perspective rather than strict abstinence and some found meditation easier to explore than concepts of a higher power in Alcoholics and Narcotics Anonymous. I met someone from this group who decorated the walls of their apartment with pictures of loved ones who had died. I followed their advice and it has been incredibly helpful in feeling a connection to loved ones lost, and many of my clients have found it helpful as well.

When I had finally felt ready to hang my own pictures, I nevertheless did not want to be exposed to them 24/7. The Toronto Buddhist Church, a Jodo Shinshu Pure Land temple, has a Butsudan Adoption program. A Butsudan is an altar common to Japanese Buddhist homes that is used for honoring Buddhas and Bodhisattvas as well as paying respects to people who have died and connecting to one's ancestors. The Toronto Buddhist Church started this adoption program so that when community members move to smaller homes, for example, older adults moving to care centres, their Butsudans can be re-used rather than being thrown away. I went to the

Toronto Buddhist Church and from their large collection, selected a Butsudan that had doors on it like a cabinet, so I could choose when I would be seeing the pictures of my loved ones. I do not feel welcome to go to family funerals due to my emancipation from my family and I am not usually told the dates for when the funerals are happening. I usually hold my own funerals for people, but, until I obtained the Butsudan, I never had a way of revisiting those who died – I never know where people's graves are. I began lighting incense and candles on a regular basis and communing with my dead relatives, my ex who killed himself, and someone who went to that same Buddhist harm reduction group I discussed earlier – who died of an opioid overdose.

Familial Homophobia, Intimate Partner Violence, Sexual Abuse, and Feminist Therapy

Sarah Schulman's (2009) work interrogates the dominant narrative that homophobia is an individual issue within families. She counters this narrative by explaining that it is in fact a cultural crisis that is enabled by a lack of societal condemnation of homophobia and family shunning practices. She explains that the family is often a queer person's first exposure to homophobia and that the affective experience of familial homophobia is so uniquely painful that even the most progressive straight people cannot relate. She discusses how liberal straight people who are accepting of gay people often fail to stand up for gay family members experiencing homophobia and will use their heterosexuality as currency within the family. She explains how lateral violence occurs within queer communities, where those queers engaged in structural activism are often seen as militant. She argues that the false relegation of familial homophobia to the private sphere enables its continued existence. Schulman explains that gay people must begin advocating for a cultural shift in which familial homophobia itself is stigmatized and seen as a public matter.

The trauma of being shunned by one's family may be obvious, but the cultural roots and consequences of this trauma are eschewed from public discourse. Schulman's work enables us to critically examine the trauma of familial homophobia on a macro scale. Schulman mentions that Parents and Friends of Lesbians and Gays (PFLAG) would be more effective in its work if it engaged in structural activism around this cultural crisis. She states that there is precedence for such a collective response from the AIDS crisis. I found community and family through the foster care system, the ballroom scene, and Buddhist sanghas, but that did not change the systemic factors that led my parents to think that it is acceptable to engage in violence and abandonment of a queer person to which they gave birth. Until these structural issues are ameliorated, this will keep happening to other queer and trans youth as well. Familial homophobia will continue to be an issue that comes up in spiritual care, and Buddhist clergy would do well to become educated on this (though one does not have to be an expert) so that they can support queer people and their relatives. Buddhist clergy set the tone for what a sangha will look like. My Zen teacher gives dharma talks every Sunday. One of those talks was during Pride about Buddhism and queerness. This sets the tone that queerphobia is unacceptable in our sangha and that she is knowledgeable enough that queer people and their families could come to her if they needed.

Feminist therapy can be immensely helpful for clients facing structural violence. Crowder (2016) discusses mindfulness-based feminist therapy in the context of intimate partner violence. She explains that both feminism and Buddhist philosophy have similar understandings of the social construction of the self and they can inform each other, the former on the issue of oppression and the latter on dis-identifying from stories of who we are, seeing ourselves as greater than what happened to us. Domestic abuse, like familial homophobia, is a challenging issue within queer communities. We hurt each other in the ways that heterosexual people hurt us.

Like familial homophobia, domestic abuse requires a structural and community response that creates the societal conditions for it to be seen as completely unacceptable rather than simply a quiet issue that happens behind closed doors. Because feminist therapy focuses on an intersectional analysis of oppression in the context

of the client's life, one therapeutic technique is encouraging collective activism. When I work with clients who have experienced
sexual violence, I encourage them to attend feminist groups run
by sexual violence organizations and to march at Take Back the
Night, the annual international protest against rape. This kind of
action also helps people feel like they are not alone. It is extremely common for survivors of violence to blame themselves, and being with other survivors can help decrease that internalized victim
blaming. Activist work can also help survivors feel like they are
doing something about what happened to them. Tonglen meditation may similarly help decrease isolation and help survivors feel
like they are doing something about what happened, as the meditation is about opening the heart to others such as survivors around
the world. The criminal punishment system offers little justice for
survivors and often does more traumatic harm than good, but activism can help survivors feel empowered on their own terms to
affect social change. Meditation can help activists arrive to protests,
sign-making parties, and meetings at their cognitive best.

Mondo Zen's Emotional Koan Practice

The first year of my Zen priest training focused heavily on Mondo
Zen's Ego Transformation and Emotional Koan practice, and I have
realized that there is something here that might be useful for queer
folks and people in spiritual care. Jun Po Denis Kelly Roshi created
this practice because he felt that some practitioners were achieving
strong advances in their practices yet were still lacking emotional
integration. We have seen the sexual indiscretions of seemingly advanced Buddhist teachers (though this is as much about power and
sexism as it is a problem of emotional intelligence), and we have
seen Buddhist teachers advocate for war. We need to ensure that
Buddhist clergy are working on themselves enough to not harm
their students. Jun Po Roshi also felt that in contemporary times,
practitioners, especially Westerners, were not resonating with East
Asian koans, some of which are from as far back as the 10th century. Here, we obviously see a form of Buddhist modernism, though

there is something to be said about an *intentional* and respectful modernization. As I understand it, Jun Po Roshi is not saying to throw out the traditional koans and is, instead, offering another koan system that people can optionally try for themselves. It is also important to highlight that, unlike some problematic forms of Buddhist modernism, he is not claiming that he is returning to some "original Buddhism," steeped in a West-is-Best narrative.

Jun Po Roshi was dharma heir to Eido Shimano. In 2010, Shimano was forced to resign from his position as head abbot of Dai Bosatsu due to decades of allegations of sexual misconduct, sexual harassment, and sexual assault (Oppenheimer, 2014). Jun Po Roshi also had an affair with a married student, shaking his sangha (Gleig & Langenberg, 2023). I do not endorse either of these teachers, and I had a difficult time deciding whether or not to include the emotional koan program here. There are many unfortunate examples of this kind of abuse at the hands of clergy across traditions. Their actions were very troubling to me as a survivor of childhood sexual abuse and as someone who narrowly escaped sexual abuse in adulthood at the hands of a monk. A closeted monk, who was not my teacher, once invited me to his temple alone and tried to sexually assault me. Clergy have a responsibility to their students and to the community as a whole. This is part of why I appreciate having a feminist teacher. Monastics are supposed to be celibate and even though unlike monastics, Zen priests like Jun Po Roshi do not necessarily take a vow of celibacy, they are still expected to uphold the precept on sexual misconduct, which includes not hurting others by having affairs and not having sexual relationships with students. I hesitantly include the emotional koan practice here, separating the teachings from who created it, because I have experienced great benefits from the practice.

The emotional koan practice involves several steps. It begins with a philosophical reorientation, helping students understand that the ego is not permanent. The ego is a conditioned process of the self-referencing mind, that part of us which involves our thoughts, feelings, emotions, and memories. It is not a self and it also maintains the illusion of the self/other distinction. The ego dies when we die, it disappears in deep sleep, and it changes over time. We are not trying to kill the ego. We are re-educating the ego so that it can be healthy rather than emotionally immature and so that it can be re-constructed, reconditioned, and informed by its understanding of its emptiness of self. We learn to move from an egocentric view to a Buddha-centric view.

The koan process involves ego transformation koans that help us access a *dhyana* consciousness that in Mondo Zen is called 'Clear Deep Heart-Mind.' This is the level of consciousness from which we want to condition ourselves to continually operate. The first ten koans focus on insight, embodiment of this insight, and the articulation of one's insight. The last three are the emotional koans. In the Mondo Zen Koan practice, thoughts and feelings are senses just like smell, touch, taste, sight, and sound; they bring us information. Rather than *re*acting from our old patterns, the emotional koans help us find the information that is in our feelings, so that we may act from deep care.

I have included the koans below. The Hollow Bones Zen community that Jun Po Roshi founded has online and in-person programs. They have facilitators, some of whom are part of Hollow Bones Zen and some of whom have started their own sanghas, who can guide you through the process. Jun Po Roshi and Keith Martin Smith (2014) co-authored *The heart of Zen: Enlightenment, emotional maturity, and what it really takes for spiritual liberation.* The book is a dialogue between the two, with an appendix that includes the koans and commentary for the koans. In addition to these 13 koans, the Mondo Zen program also uses the Wu Koan. There was a dialogue where Chinese Zen master Zhaozhou was asked, "does a dog have Buddha nature?" and he answered "Wu," meaning, "no". This was a paradox because according to Mahayana Buddhist thought, all beings have Buddha nature. Inspired by this koan, Mondo Zen uses the Know/No Koan or Kata, which can applied in daily life. No to the habitual reaction and knowing the deeper truth of who we are – clear, deep, heart-mind. Each of the koans can ride the breath. One might use a heart-centered concentration meditation, where the koans are breathed in and out of one's heart-centre.

Mondo Zen Ego Transformation and
Emotional Awareness Intervention Koans

- Is it possible to just purely listen without an opinion?
- Where within your body is the center of this deeper listening located?
- Who are you, who am I, who are we, within this deep, heart-felt listening?
- What is the difference between "I Don't Know" and "Not Knowing"?
- What are you like, what are we like, at this depth of consciousness?
- Express your new insight with a silent gesture of embodied consciousness.
- Use a signifier and your name to recall Clear Deep Heart-Mind. Respond with this awareness.
- Does this Clear Deep Heart-Mind come and go?
- Now that you have experienced Clear Deep Heart-Mind, what must you do to bring this realization forth right now and at any time in your daily life?
- What feelings arise when you actually experience this insight and understanding?
- What are the deeper feelings that lie beneath violent anger, shame, and disconnection?
- Now that you know the deeper feelings beneath these violent emotive reactions, can anyone or anything ever make you violently angry, shame you, or make you disconnect/dissociate?
- Select a recurring negative habitual reaction from your daily life and transform it into a conscious, compassionate response. Visualize yourself transforming a habitual negative reaction into a conscious, compassionate response (Hollow Bones Zen, 2021).

These koans have been incredibly valuable to me in my own growth out of reactive patterns. They might be helpful for other queer folks as well. They can certainly be used in Buddhist spiritual care programs to help practitioners and clients achieve deep insight into their own Clear Deep Heart-Mind and to be able to overcome conditioned reactions. There may be a place for this koan program in psychotherapy, although, that is something that I would need to think through more deeply before offering suggestions. Some of the insights around the deeper feelings beneath our challenging emotions definitely have a place in counselling.

Practice

R.A.I.N. of Self-Compassion Meditation for Difficult Emotions

Self-compassion is a means of relating to difficulty with kindness. This is similar to to the psychotherapeutic concept of uncondition-al positive regard, popularized by Carl Rogers (1951), but rather than being directed towards a client, it is directed toward oneself. Self-compassion is much different than self-esteem. Self-esteem in-volves directing praise toward oneself for ego-based achievements or status. Self-compassion is the development of unconditional love toward the self. Kristin Neff and Christopher Germer (2018) are prominent authors credited for galvanizing self-compassion re-search and literature in the Western world. This has also become a central part of Compassion-Focused Therapy.

Self-compassion involves three components:
- Mindfulness – this interpretation of mindfulness involves present time awareness.
- Self-kindness – a sense of love and warmth directed toward the self in the face of hardship, rather than criticism.
- Common humanity – a recognition that suffering is part of the universal experience of all sentient beings.

R.A.I.N. meditations are a way that one can practice self-compassion in the midst of difficulty. R.A.I.N. is an acronym that is used in numerous Buddhist circles. There are some variations to the acro-nym. The version that we'll be exploring can be credited to the author, Tara Brach (2017). After learning this approach in therapy, it has continued to be one of the strongest practices in my life for processing difficult emotions. I use it a lot with therapy clients and I have taught countless workshops on R.A.I.N., with groups from children with disabilities in Germany to queer and trans refugee claimants in Canada, and regardless of the group, it seems to have strong benefits for a lot of people.

R.A.I.N. stands for:
- Recognize
- Allow
- Investigate the bodily sensations
- Nourish with self-compassion

Start with awareness of the breath, as a means of grounding. Notice the inhale and the exhale for a few minutes.

Once you feel ready, let a challenging circumstance come to mind. Allow your mind to wander into the details of this circumstance for a moment.

Next, notice what feelings come up. Try to label these emotions. Perhaps anger is present. Perhaps fear is knocking at the door. This is the R of R.A.I.N., recognizing. Often, there will be multiple feelings present – make space for that. Rather than saying "I am sad," try "sadness is present," for example, or "there's some anger here." This is important because we are not our emotions. Our emotions are information just like any other sense and are due to our conditioning..

Once you've identified the feelings that are coming up, dedicate some time to allowing them to be there. Simply bear witness to these feelings. It can help to mentally say, "yes," to these emotions. Practice inviting them in for tea, perhaps even encouraging them to be there.

After you've invited the emotions in, you'll likely notice some sensations in the body. This brings us to the I of R.A.I.N., investigation. This is not an investigation of the story behind the situation, it is simply a physical investigation of feelings in the body. You might feel sadness in a certain part of the body. What does it feel like? Is it tight in the throat? Perhaps it is a burning in the chest. Try to let this feeling manifest however it needs to in the body.

Finally, we move to the N of R.A.I.N., nourishing with self-compassion. For this part of the meditation, you might place your hand on your heart. Alternatively, you might place your hand on another part of the body where you feel the emotion. Try to send love and warmth to yourself. Mentally say to yourself a kind phrase, like, "it's okay, it's hard to feel this, and that's okay." Spend some time consoling yourself.

Once you feel that you have given the emotion adequate attention, remember that you are not alone. There are countless people around the world feeling this same difficult emotion, maybe with similar or different circumstances. Send out compassion to all beings everywhere who feel this way. This is the common humanity piece of self-compassion. While not all beings experience the same circumstances as you, everyone, everywhere, experiences these emotions.

To end the meditation, spend some time grounding yourself. It is important to take some time to bring your attention back to the breath for a few minutes.

7

Precarious Love:
On Interconnectedness for a
Queer(ed) and Trans(formed) Engaged Buddhism

Intersectionality has become an integral part of queer movements and has entered even mainstream queer consciousness as we understand that queer movements must also tackle other forms of marginalization to successfully enhance the social conditions for everyone, not just the privileged few. Intersectionality emerged from Black feminist critique as a form of social analysis that considers how oppressions are mutually reinforcing and interlocking (Dhamoon, 2011) during a time when dominant feminist praxis universalized white experiences of womanhood. Often it is misunderstood as a summative approach to oppression that seeks to discern the most oppressed person in the room. Instead, intersectionality is more concerned with how oppressions manifest themselves differently depending on the multiple locations of the oppressed and how techniques of marginalization are mutually constituting; for one form of hegemony to end, all must end. This idea echoes the bodhisattva vow to apply their enlightened compassion to all suffering until there is no sentient being left suffering. It is from this point that I wish to springboard a conclusion to this book by exploring the necropolitical maldistribution of inequity and how Buddhist work on the transcendence of the self/other dichotomy can encourage an understanding of interconnectedness that is politically and spiritually useful in queer Buddhist studies.

Judith Butler's (2016) conceptualization of precarity "as the politically induced condition that would deny equal exposure through the radically unequal distribution of wealth and the different ways of exposing certain populations, racially and nationally conceptualized, to greater violence" (Butler, 2016, p. 28) can be used to unearth the uneven distribution of oppression in queer necropolitical times. Butler (2004) uses the term 'precarity' differently than 'precarious.' Butlerian precariousness is "a feature of all life" (Butler, 2016, p. 25) as a result of our reliance on others to survive, much like the First Noble Truth identifies suffering as part of existence. In juxtaposition, her use of 'precarity' is a state of "maximized precariousness for populations exposed to arbitrary violence who often have no other option than to appeal to the very state from which they need protection" (Butler, 2016, p. 26). Here, we see how multiply marginalized queers, those who may experience racialized violence in addition to queerphobia, homelessness, and other challenges, are in extreme states of precarity in which they must appeal to the hearts of the oppressors for help, the very people who rule a system that was created to systematically disadvantage them in the first place. Discursive frames determine our affective responses to death, deeming some lives grievable, worthy of mourning, and others ungrievable (Butler, 2016). The former must be valued and understood as a life in the first place. The extensive theoretical work on queer suffering explored in this book affirms the notion that queers are well attuned to the noble truth of suffering. I propose that part of the way out of this suffering is to recognize our shared interests in ending the precarity of the most marginalized queers through coalitional activism that recognizes the interconnectedness of oppressions.

Queer-sattvas and Trans-sattvas in Socially Engaged Buddhism

Since engaged Buddhism rarely overtly discusses queerphobia, I propose that a queer engaged Buddhism start its work using trans law professor Dean Spade's (2015) framework of trickle-up social justice praxis. Much of early trans politics focused on benefiting the more privileged, white, binary trans people, with the idea that the fruits of such activism would eventually trickle down to the multiply marginalized, the same notion that motivates homonormative queer activism. Dean Spade (2015) coined trickle-up social justice praxis as a framework that puts the concerns of the multiply marginalized first with the knowledge that by benefiting, for example, poor, impoverished, imprisoned, and/or racialized trans people, more privileged trans people will inevitably benefit and this will lead to a more equitable distribution of life chances, or in Butlerian words, a less precarity, for all. It is here that the *brahma vihara* (divine abode, or immeasurable quality) of *karuna* (compassion) can be most productively developed. If we are to transcend the distinction between my needs and the needs of others and to instead focus on whose needs are particularly pressing, we can benefit a larger quantity of beings.

Fuller (2021) explains that there is a long history of using bodhisattvas to galvanize activism in engaged Buddhism. He proposes the utility of the queer-sattva or trans-sattva as a potential for furthering queer and trans engaged Buddhism. Fuller (2021) goes on to explain how queer and trans Buddhists have referred to the *Mettā Sutta* (*Lovingkindness Sutta*) in our pleas to the cisgender, heterosexual community that we just want to be treated with the basic Buddhist value of lovingkindness. Fuller (2021) discusses how in the *Aggañña Sutta* (D III 80-98) it is said that at the beginning of this world's cyclic existence there were no sexes and genders; these methods of categorization arose due to greed and desire (D III 88). This does not mean that we should treat trans people as if they are full of greed and desire any more than cis people, rather, it is a story about the creation of a dualistic system that does not work for a lot of people. This story about a time before gender sounds like a trans utopia to me as a non-binary person. But just like Kate Bornstein stated in the 2016 talk I referenced earlier in this book, gender is not going away anytime soon, so we should have fun with it.

What is a queer-sattva or a trans-sattva? I do not wish to prescribe a definition, as I think that this is something queer folks and communities should define for themselves, and such notions could change over time. I will say that I have often felt as though queer people are gifted with the ability to see things in the world to which cisgender, heterosexual people are often blind. It is sometimes as if we gain access to rainbow-coloured glasses that, if we choose to put them, on, allows us to see the hidden problematic norms around gender and sexuality in our world. Sometimes these glasses can feel like a burden, overwhelming us, as we get tired of seeing these challenges all the time. Instead of taking them off, we can connect with other people in our community, gain emotional support from other queer people, and educate non-queer folks and those queer folks who haven't put on their rainbow glasses, to be able to understand the structural roots of difficulties such as familial homophobia and cissexism. We can use practices like tonglen to open our heart rather than close it during difficult times and to connect with the suffering of other queer beings. We can work from a trickle-up social justice praxis to aid other queer people who are suffering. We can use lovingkindness to help us soften our reactions to those who harm us. We can use the Mondo Zen Koan practice's emotional koans to help us respond to the world from Clear Deep (Rainbow) Heart-Mind.

We can create our own utopia in the here and now, one that is grounded in an affect of play and joy, like the joy that I experienced while writing this book. We can do this by strengthening our queer and trans Buddhist communities. When we feel like losing hope, we can arouse a queer bodhicitta, that awakened heart-mind's intention to help other suffering beings. Many people find helping others to be a powerful antidote to their depression. Feminist therapy encourages us to engage in consciousness raising as a form of empowerment, of doing something about our oppression, and of connecting to other people who have experienced the same harm as us. Queer bodhicitta can help us strengthen our altruistic intentions and live in the world as queer-sattvas and trans-sattvas. I hope that this book contributes to a long line of future queer-sattva and trans-sattva work, activism, and care, which takes metta as the garden from which our movement grows.

References

Abé, R. (2015). Revisiting the Dragon Princess: Her role in medieval Engi stories and their implications in reading the Lotus Sutra. *Japanese Journal of Religious Studies, 42*(1), 27–70.

Ahmed, S. (2006). *Queer phenomenology: Orientations, objects, others.* Duke University Press.

_____. (2010). *The promise of happiness.* Duke University Press.

Anālayo, B. (2019). Adding historical depth to definitions of mindfulness. *Current Opinion in Psychology, 28,* 11–14.

_____. (2020). The myth of McMindfulness. *Mindfulness, 11*(2), 472–479.

_____. (2022). Situating mindfulness, part 2: Early Buddhist soteriology. *Mindfulness, 13*(4), 855–862.

Artinger, B. G. (2021). On Pāli Vinaya conceptions of sex and precedents for transgender ordination. *Journal of Buddhist Ethics, 28*(1), 295–338.

Atlas, C. (2019). Gender and emptiness. In K. Manders & E. Marston (Eds.), *Transcending: Trans Buddhist voices* (pp. 133–145). North Atlantic Books.

Bailey, C. (2009). Embracing the icon: The feminist potential of the trans bodhisattva, Kuan Yin. *Hypatia, 24*(3), 178–196.

Baker, D. (2010). Return of the eunuch: Gender disobedience as a path to awakening in Buddhist tantra. *Postscripts: The Journal of Sacred Texts and Contemporary Worlds, 4*(3), 339–366.

Balkwill, S. (2021). Disappearing and disappeared daughters in medieval Chinese Buddhism: Sūtras on sex transformation and an intervention into their transmission history. *History of Religions, 60*(4), 255–286.

Beachy, R. (2014). *Gay Berlin: Birthplace of a modern identity.* Knopf.

Blosnich, J. R., Henderson, E.R., Coulter, R. W. S., Goldbach, J.T., & Meyer, I.H. (2020). Sexual orientation change efforts, adverse childhood experiences, and suicide ideation and attempt among sexual minority adults, United States, 2016–2018.

American Journal of Public Health, 110(7), 1024–1030.

Bodhi, B. (1998). Dhamma and non-duality. *Access to Insight.* https://www.accesstoinsight.org/lib/authors/bodhi/bps-essay_27.html

_____. (2010). Arahants, bodhisattvas, and buddhas. *Access to Insight.* https://www.accesstoinsight.org/lib/authors/bodhi/arahantsbodhisattvas.html

_____. (2013). What does mindfulness really mean? A canonical perspective. In J.M.G. Williams & J. Kabat-Zinn (Eds.), *Mindfulness: Diverse perspectives on its meaning, origins, and applications* (pp. 19–39). Routledge.

Bornstein, K. (1994). *Gender outlaw: On men, women and the rest of us.* Vintage Books.

_____. (2013). *My new gender workbook: A step-by-step guide to achieving world peace through gender anarchy and sex positivity* (Rev. ed.). Routledge.

Boucher, S. (2000). *Discovering Kwan Yin: Buddhist goddess of compassion.* Beacon Press.

Brach, T. (2017). The RAIN of Self-Compassion: A simple practice for clients and clinicians. In J. Loizzo., M. Neale., E. Wolf. (Eds.), *Advances in contemplative psychotherapy* (pp. 146-154). Routledge.

Buckner, R. (2020). Zen in distress: Theorizing gender dysphoria and traumatic remembrance within Sōtō Zen meditation. *Religions, 11*(11), 1–14.

Butler, J. (1991). Imitation and gender subordination. In D. Fuss (Ed.), *Inside/out: Lesbian theories, gay theories* (pp. 13–31). Routledge.

_____. (2004). *Precarious life: The powers of mourning and violence.* Verso.

_____. (2016). *Frames of war: When is life grievable?* Verso.

_____. (2020). Performative acts and gender constitution: An essay in phenomenology and feminist theory. In C.R. McCann & S.-K. Kim (Eds.), *Feminist theory reader: Local and global perspectives* (5th ed., pp. 353–361). Routledge.

Cabezón, J.I. (1993). Homosexuality and Buddhism. In A. Swidler

(Ed.), *Homosexuality and world religions* (pp. 81–101). Trinity Press International.

_____. (1998). Homosexuality and Buddhism. In W. Leyland (Ed.), *Queer Dharma: Voices of gay Buddhists* (Vol. 1, pp. 29–44). Gay Sunshine Press.

_____. (2017). *Sexuality in classical South Asian Buddhism.* Simon & Schuster.

Caruth, C. (1995). *Trauma: Explorations in memory.* Johns Hopkins University Press.

Chödrön, P. (2001). *Start where you are: A guide to compassionate living.* Shambhala Publications.

_____ (2016). *When things Fall apart: Heart advice for difficult times.* Shambhala

Chödrön, B.T. (2005). *Cultivating a compassionate heart: The yoga method of Chenrezig.* Shambhala Publications.

Cohen, H., Neumann, L., Haiman, Y., Matar, M.A., Press, J., & Buskila, D. (2002). Prevalence of post-traumatic stress disorder in fibromyalgia patients: Overlapping syndromes or post-traumatic fibromyalgia syndrome? *Seminars in Arthritis and Rheumatism, 32*(1), 38–50.

Coleman, J. W. (2001). *The New Buddhism: The Western Transformation of an Ancient Tradition.* London: Oxford University Press.

Conkin, D. (1998). The Dalai Lama and Gay Love. In W. Leyland (Ed). *Queer Dharma: Voices of gay Buddhists, Volume 1* (pp.351-56). Gay Sunshine Press.

Conrad, R. (2014). *Against equality: Queer revolution, not mere inclusion.* AK Press.

Corless, R.J. (1998). Coming out in the sangha: Queer community in American Buddhism. In C.S. Prebish & K.K. Tanaka (Eds.), *The faces of Buddhism in America* (pp. 253–265). University of California Press.

_____. (2004). Towards a queer dharmology of sex. *Culture and Religion, 5*(2), 229–243.

Crompton, L. (2003). *Homosexuality and civilization.* Harvard University Press.

Crowder, R. (2016). Mindfulness-based feminist therapy: The intermingling edges of self-compassion and social justice. *Journal of Religion & Spirituality in Social Work: Social Thought, 35*(1–2), 24–40.

Cvetkovich, A. (2003). *An archive of feelings: Trauma, sexuality, and lesbian public cultures.* Duke University Press.

_____. (2012). *Depression: A public feeling.* Duke University Press.

Dhamoon, R.K. (2011). Considerations on mainstreaming intersectionality. *Political Research Quarterly, 64*(1), 230–243.

Drolma, L.P. (2019). *Love on every breath: Tonglen meditation for transforming pain into joy.* New World Library.

Enke, F. (2019). What is a body, anyway? Form, deep listening, and compassion on a Buddhist trans path. In K. Manders & E. Marston (Eds.), *Transcending: Trans Buddhist voices* (pp. 197–208). North Atlantic Books.

Epstein, M. (2008). *Psychotherapy without the self: A Buddhist perspective.* Yale University Press.

Foucault, M. (1990). *The history of sexuality: An introduction, volume I.* Trans. Robert Hurley. Vintage.

Freccero, C. (2013). Queer spectrality: Haunting the past. In G.E. Haggerty, & M. McGarry (Eds.), *The spectralities reader: Ghosts and haunting in contemporary cultural theory* (pp. 335–359). Bloomsbury Academic.

Fuller, P. (2021). *An introduction to engaged Buddhism.* Bloomsbury Academic.

Garfield, J. (2002). *Empty words: Buddhist philosophy and cross-cultural interpretation.* Oxford University Press.

Gleig, A. (2012). Queering Buddhism or Buddhist de-queering? Reflecting on differences amongst Western LGBTQI Buddhists and the limits of liberal convert Buddhism. *Theology & Sexuality, 18*(3), 198–214.

_____. (2019). *American dharma: Buddhism beyond modernity.* Yale University Press.

_____., & Langenberg, A. P. (2023). Sexual ethics and healthy boundaries in the wake of teacher abuse. *Buddhadharma: Lion's*

Roar. https://www.lionsroar.com/sexual-ethics-and-healthy-boundaries-in-the-wake-of-teacher-abuse/

Global News. (2022, July 15). Monkeypox: With cases jumping 59% in Canada, what are the signs you need to know? [Video]. *YouTube*. https://www.youtube.com/watch?v=GiSRxy5sSjo

Gombrich, R. (2009). *Theravāda Buddhism: A social history from ancient Benares to modern Colombo* (2nd ed.). Routledge.

Gyatso, J. (2003). One plus one makes three: Buddhist gender, monasticism, and the law of the non-excluded middle. *History of Religions, 43*, 89–115.

Haiku of the Forest. (2014, August 18). Side note: Homosexuality in Japan & haiku. *Haiku of the Forest*. https://haikuoftheforest.wordpress.com/2014/08/18/side-note-homosexuality-in-japan-haiku/comment-page-1/

Harvey, P. (2000). *An introduction to Buddhist ethics: Foundations, values and issues*. Cambridge University Press.

Harrold, R. (2019). *My Buddha is pink: Buddhism from a LGBTQI perspective*. Sumeru Press.

Hawa, F. (2018, December). Lady Gaga's speech on Elle women award: Theme and stylistic levels. *Proceedings of the International Conference on English Language Teaching (INACELT), 2*(1), 88–99.

Hollow Bones Zen. (2021). *Mondo Zen: Ego transformation koans, emotional awareness koans*. https://hollowboneszen.org/wp-content/uploads/2023/01/Hollow-Bones-Zen-Mondo-Zen-Manual.pdf

Heng-ching Shih. (1994). *The Sutra on Upāsaka Precepts* (C. Chun-fang, Trans.). Numata Center for Buddhist Translation and Research.

Hu, H.-L. (2019). The white feminism in Rita Gross' critique of gender identities and reconstruction of Buddhism. In G. Yancy & E. McRae (Eds.), *Buddhism and whiteness* (pp. 293–308). Lexington Books.

Jackson, P.A. (1995). Thai Buddhist accounts of male homosexuality and AIDS in the 1980s. *The Australian Journal of Anthropology, 6*(1–2), 140–153.

Kerry, S. (2021, November). Australian LGBTQIA+ Buddhists. Paper presented at the 1st International Queer Buddhist Conference (online).

Kreitzer, R.J., & Sweet-Cushman, J. (2022). Evaluating student evaluations of teaching: A review of measurement and equity bias in SETs and recommendations for ethical reform. *Journal of Academic Ethics, 20*(4), 709–720.

Levman, B. (2019). The language the Buddha spoke. *Journal of the Oxford Centre for Buddhist Studies, 17*, 63-105.

Li, R. (2023). *Illumination: A Guide to the Method of No-Method.* Shambhala Publications.

Liu, W. (2017). Toward a queer psychology of affect: Restarting from shameful places. *Subjectivity, 10*(1), 44–62.

Lopez Jr., D.S. (2009). *Buddhism and science: A guide for the perplexed.* University of Chicago Press.

Love, H. (2009). *Feeling backward: Loss and the politics of queer history.* Harvard University Press.

Manuel, Z.E. (2015). *The way of tenderness: Awakening through race, sexuality, and gender.* Wisdom Publications.

Mbembé, A. (2003). Necropolitics (L. Meintjes, Trans.). *Public Culture, 15*(1), 11–40.

McMahan, D.L. (2008). *The making of Buddhist modernism.* Oxford University Press.

Morrigan, C. (2017). Trauma time: The queer temporalities of the traumatized mind. *Somatechnics, 7*(1), 50–58.

Muncaster, K. (2021a, March 16). Compassionate queers part 2: Rainbow Tonglen with Kody Muncaster [Video]. *Rainbodhi.* https://www.youtube.com/watch?v=MPZnUCQdqIc&t=775s

_____. (2021b). PrEP will not save us: The ghosts of AIDS and suicide. In M. B. Sycamore (Ed.), *Between certain death and a possible future: Queer writing on growing up with the AIDS crisis* (pp. 296–301). Arsenal Pulp Press.

_____. (2022). Towards a queer Buddhist hermeneutics: Reparative readings of queer and trans Buddhist histories. In J. Admans & D. Valentin (Eds.), *Beyond worship* (pp. 54–70). Riverdale Avenue Books.

_____. (2023). Queerly mad: Cripping grief and post-traumatic fibromyalgia syndrome. In S. Chatterjee & P. H. Lee (Eds.), *Plural feminisms: Narrativising resistance as everyday praxis* (pp. 134–149). Bloomsbury Academic.

_____. (2025). Queer, trans, and intersex Buddhism: Implications for culturally relevant social work practice. *Journal of Religion & Spirituality in Social Work: Social Thought, 44*(2), 1-18.

Muncaster, K., Masterman, C., Barnett, T., Kozak, R. A., Mandel, E., Campbell, K., & Biondi MJ, M. J. (2024). A retrospective chart review and thematic analysis of patients seeking mpox vaccination during the initial outbreak in 2022–2023: evaluation of access, motivations, and stigma. *BMC Public Health, 24*(1), 34–36.

Muñoz, J.E. (2019). *Cruising utopia: The then and there of queer futurity*. NYU Press.

Neff, K., & Germer, C. (2018). *The mindful self-compassion workbook: A proven way to accept yourself, build inner strength, and thrive*. Guilford Publications.

Nhat Hanh, T. (1967). *Vietnam: Lotus in the sea of fire*. Hill and Wang.

Norbu, N.T. (2020). *A guide to the thirty-seven practices of a bodhisattva* (C. Stagg, Trans.). Shambhala Publications.

Ocha, W. (2023). Buddhism, gender, and sexualities: Queer spiritualities in Thailand. *Equality, Diversity and Inclusion: An International Journal, 42*(5), 685–705.

Oppenheimer, M. December 18, 2014. The Zen Predator of the Upper East Side, *The Atlantic*.

Owens, L.R. (2020). *Love and rage: The path of liberation through anger*. North Atlantic Books.

_____. (2021, April 2). Becoming a queer bodhisattva with Lama Rod Owens: Rainbodhi online [Video]. *YouTube*. https://www.youtube.com/watch?v=KdHH3pLiKUo&t=1472s

Pascoe, C.J. (2011). *Dude, you're a fag: Masculinity and sexuality in high school* (2nd ed.). University of California Press.

Parker, L.L., & Harriger, J.A. (2020). Eating disorders and

disordered eating behaviors in the LGBT population: A review of the literature. *Journal of Eating Disorders, 8*(51), 1–20.

Perreault, Y., Fitton, W., & McGovern, M. (2010). The presence of absence: Bereavement in long-term survivors of multiple AIDS-related losses. *Bereavement Care, 29*(3), 26-33.

Piepzna-Samarasinha, L.L. (2018). *Care work: Dreaming disability justice.* Arsenal Pulp Press.

Puar, J.K. (2006). Mapping US homonormativities. *Gender, Place & Culture, 13*(1), pp.67-88.

_____. (2017). *Terrorist assemblages: Homonationalism in queer times* (2nd ed.). Duke University Press.

Queen, C.S. (1996). Introduction: The shapes and sources of engaged Buddhism. In C.S. Queen & S. B. King (Eds.), *Engaged Buddhism: Buddhist liberation movements in Asia* (pp. 1–44). State University of New York Press.

Reeves, G. (2008). *The Lotus Sutra.* Wisdom Publications.

Riach, K., Rumens, N., & Tyler, M. (2014). Un/doing chrononormativity: Negotiating ageing, gender and sexuality in organizational life. *Organization Studies, 35*(11), 1677–1698.

Rogers, C. R. (1951). *Client-centered therapy: Its current practice, implications, and theory.* Boston: Houghton Mifflin.

Roshi, J.P.D.K., & Martin-Smith, K. (2014). *The heart of Zen: Enlightenment, emotional maturity, and what it really takes for spiritual liberation.* North Atlantic Books.

Scherer, B. (2006). Gender transformed and meta-gendered enlightenment: Reading Buddhist narratives as paradigms of inclusiveness. *Revista de Estudos da Religião, 3,* 65–76.

_____. (2021). Queering Buddhist traditions. In *Oxford Research Encyclopedia of Religion.* https://doi.org/10.1093/acrefore/9780199340378.013.881

Sweet, M.J. (2000). Pining away for the sight of the handsome Cobra King: Ananda as gay ancestor and role model. In W. Leyland (Ed.), *Queer Dharma: Voices of gay Buddhists* (Vol. 2, pp. 13–24). Gay Sunshine Press.

Schneider, D. (2020). *Street Zen: The life and work of Issan Dorsey.* Shambhala Publications.

Schulman, S. (2009). *Ties that bind: Familial homophobia and its consequences*. The New Press.

Sedgwick, E.K. (1993). *Tendencies*. Duke University Press.

_____. (2003). *Touching feeling: Affect, pedagogy, performativity*. Duke University Press.

Spade, D. (2015). *Normal life: Administrative violence, critical trans politics, and the limits of law* (2nd ed.). Duke University Press.

Sycamore, M.B. (Ed.). (2010). *Nobody passes: Rejecting the rules of gender and conformity*. Seal Press.

Tedeschi, R.G., & Calhoun, L.G. (2004). Posttraumatic growth: Conceptual foundations and empirical evidence. *Psychological Inquiry, 15*(1), 1–18.

Thompson, E. (2020). *Why I am not a Buddhist*. Yale University Press.

Vimala, B. (2021). Through the yellow gate: Ordination of gender-nonconforming people in the Buddhist Vinaya. *Sutta Central*. https://discourse.suttacentral.net/t/through-the-yellow-gate-ordination-of-gender-nonconforming-people-in-the-buddhist-vinaya/18752

Vincent, B. (2020). *Non-binary genders: Navigating communities, identities, and healthcare*. Policy Press.

Watson, B. (1997). *The Vimalakirti Sutra*. Columbia University Press.

Wilson, J. (2012). "All beings are equally embraced by Amida Buddha": Jodo Shinshu Buddhism and same-sex marriage in the United States. *Journal of Global Buddhism, 13*, 31–59.

Zwilling, L. (1992). Homosexuality as seen in Indian Buddhist texts. In J.I. Cabezón (Ed.), *Buddhism, sexuality, and gender* (pp. 203–214). State University of New York Press.

www.ingramcontent.com/pod-product-compliance
Lightning Source LLC
Chambersburg PA
CBHW031445280326
41927CB00037B/362